INTERNATIONAL RELATIONS DIVISION

African Development and Europe

African Development and Europe

REPORT OF A SEMINAR OF THE INTERNATIONAL STUDENT MOVEMENT FOR THE UNITED NATIONS
Cambridge, March 1966

Edited by

PETER TREGEAR AND JOHN BURLEY

With a Message from U Thant, Secretary-General of the United Nations

THE QUEEN'S AWARD TO INDUSTRY 1966

PERGAMON PRESS

OXFORD · LONDON · EDINBURGH · NEW YORK
TORONTO · SYDNEY · PARIS · BRAUNSCHWEIG

Pergamon Press Ltd., Headington Hill Hall, Oxford
4 & 5 Fitzroy Square, London W.1
Pergamon Press (Scotland) Ltd., 2 & 3 Teviot Place, Edinburgh 1
Pergamon Press Inc., Maxwell House, Fairview Park, Elmsford, New York 10523
Pergamon of Canada Ltd., 207 Queen's Quay West, Toronto 1
Pergamon Press (Aust.) Pty. Ltd., 19a Boundary Street, Rushcutters Bay, N.S.W. 2011, Australia
Pergamon Press S.A.R.L., 24 rue des Écoles, Paris 5e
Vieweg & Sohn GmbH, Burgplatz 1, Braunschweig

First edition 1970
Library of Congress Catalog Card No. 78-99989

Printed in Great Britain by The European Printing Company, Bletchley

08 006670 4 (flexicover)
08 006669 0 (hard cover)

Contents

Message from the Secretary-General of the United Nations, U Thant

INTERNATIONAL discussion and action now more positively than ever place the problem of underdevelopment second in importance only to that of disarmament. The two problems are, of course, interrelated, although not by so simple an equation as is sometimes presented by those who would like to believe that the developed nations as a whole would feel able to devote, to the economic and social development of other countries, resources as large as they now expand beyond their frontiers on their systems of military security.

In any event, it is gratifying to observe that our relatively slow progress towards disarmament has not prevented an impressive measure of mobilisation for international action on problems of development during the past several years. While there is a lack of sufficient resources actually available for such action, considerable progress has been made in terms of basic agreements, organisations, methods and techniques, and the acquisition of practical experience.

Within the United Nations system itself we possess and indeed are expanding well-established facilities, on virtually a world-wide scale, for technical assistance, pre-investment activities and development finance. These operate mainly, on the one hand, through the concerted endeavours of the United Nations and its associated agencies in what is now known as the United Nations Development Programme (UNDP) and, on the other hand, through the World Bank group of institutions and the International Monetary Fund. All of these programmes are planned and implemented with an increasing, although by no means yet perfected, degree of co-ordination among themselves and with the external assistance being provided from other sources, especially under bilateral agreements. International co-operation within the United Nations is also bringing new facilities into being and, aside from the possibilities of bolder international action suggested by the United Nations Conference on Trade and Development (UNCTAD), the multi-lateralisation of food aid through the World Food Programme, the regionalisation of development banking exemplified by the recent establishment of the African Development Bank, and the increased emphasis placed on assistance in industrial development are happenings of historical importance.

The countries of Europe, taken together, are a large and vital source of the funds, equipment and skilled manpower which support both multilateral and bilateral forms of assistance to the developing countries, as well as of the aid, trade and investment policies and practices which affect development. And the nations and territories of Africa have become, especially since the pace of emergence to independence quickened around 1960, one of the principal areas of the application of development assistance. They now receive, for example, approximately one-third of the resources available with the United Nations system for technical and pre-investment assistance.

When account is taken also of the extent of present and potential development investment in the private sector, it is clear that a substantial tangible context exists for the examination by this Seminar of the relationships between African development and Europe. There is also a less tangible but perhaps more critical side to the picture. This is comprised of such questions as that of the impact of development on African societies and on their relationships with Europe; the political effects and implications of that impact; and the adequacy or otherwise of present development efforts in terms not only of volume but also of quality and kind, and in the light also of the need to promote peace and freedom as well as better living conditions.

All of this constitutes, indeed, an important field for exploration and discussion, and I wish the Seminar a useful journey through it.

Foreword

THE first UN Development Decade—which is drawing to a close—has not been a spectacular success. In Africa, in particular, results have been disappointing and very few African countries have achieved the central target of the decade of an annual, sustainable increase of 5% per annum in total output by 1969. The African performance is specially disappointing since many of the African countries are economically, among the least developed in the world; and the challenge to Africa, Europe and the World is that of insuring much more impressive results in the second Development Decade.

If the 1970s are to be productive of more rapid economic advance, some thought has to be given to the lessons of the 1960s. Above all, it should be accepted that in the earlier decade the Africans expected too much too quickly from political independence, and the Europeans too much from the mere transfer of capital resources. Fortunately, it is now widely recognized that the process of growth and development is more complex than was earlier thought. In these circumstances, a premium attaches to wide-ranging and careful discussion of African questions; and the present book could not have been more timely.

It was not, of course, to be expected that all problems would be solved within the compass of a single seminar; nor that all that was said would command universal support. Two things, however, may be said: the choice of topics was commendably pertinent and judicious; and both papers and discussions were characterized by candour and vigour. The book thus represents an extremely useful contribution to what must be a continuing debate and discussion.

Addis Ababa

R. K. A. GARDINER

Introduction

To a very great extent, the study of the problems facing the developing countries is a response to events in these countries since independence. Nowhere is this more so than in sub-Sahara Africa over the last decade. In addition, the study has been accompanied to an ever-increasing extent by the use of interdisciplinary techniques. It is now realised, for example, that economic growth cannot be fostered simply by raising the rate of capital accumulation, or by raising the savings ratio, but that it is affected by non-economic factors such as the institutional framework, and the underlying social and political forces at work in the particular society. Much insight into the problems of development can be gained by adopting an approach which lays greater emphasis on social factors than has been the case in the past, and in particular which compares both theory and practice at each level of analysis. Moreover, within the specific field of economics as taught in Western institutions, the implicit assumption is always that the economics of development is a special case of the economics of growth, using the same tools of analysis, and formulating to a great extent the same policy implications. It is therefore instructive to contrast these views with the opinions and ideas of students educated in institutions in the developing countries.

Against this background, and under the auspices of the International Student Movement for the United Nations (ISMUN), the United Nations Student Association (UNSA) arranged a Seminar on 'African Development and Europe'. Whilst the general theme of the Seminar is clear—in its broadest sense the role and function of Europe in a developing Africa—there were a number of ways in which this could be approached. Eventually it was felt desirable to have a number of addresses on specific aspects of the problems under discussion—agricultural and industrial development, trading and administrative problems—and then to invite the participants to consider in more general terms various fields of Afro-European co-operation: rural development, technological co-operation, and political relationships. About seventy students attended the Seminar, with an equal number of European and African participants. A number of French-speaking Africans attended the Seminar, and this, together with the fact that a large number of the participants were post-graduate students, ensured that the discussions were comprehensive and informed.

The Seminar was most fortunate in being addressed by speakers who had all been engaged at close quarters with the problems on which they spoke. The relevance of their contributions was clearly reflected in the length and vehemence of the discussions which followed their speeches. We are most grateful to them for so willingly devoting their time to the Seminar, and in particular to those who travelled from abroad: M. d'Arboussier from New York, M. Pepy from Paris, and Dr. van der Vaeren from Brussels.

An event of this kind cannot be held without a great deal of work and co-operation from a number of people and organizations. We were most grateful to the following for agreeing to act as sponsors:

Alhaji ABDUL-MALIKI, then High Commissioner of Nigeria to the U.K.

A.Ll. ARMITAGE, Vice-Chancellor of the University of Cambridge.

William CLARK, Director, Overseas Development Institute, London.

Professor Daryl FORDE, University College, London.

Robert GARDINER, Executive Secretary, UN Economic Commission for Africa.

Ald. H. G. IVES, His Worship the Mayor of Cambridge.

E. N. van KLEFFENS, Chief Representative, European Coal and Steel Community.

Rt. Hon. Kenneth YOUNGER, Director, Royal Institute of International Affairs.

In addition, to advise and guide the programme and organization an Advisory Committee, with P. S. Tregear as Chairman, was established. We are most grateful in particular to Dr. Soper (Overseas

Development Institute) and Professor Shils and Dr. Richards (of Cambridge) who were most helpful, both seen and unseen, in many ways. Other members of the Committee, to whom we offer our sincerest appreciation, were Professors J. Blondel, G. Goodwin, L. J. Lewis and D. Low, and Patrick Keatley, F. J. Parkinson and David Williams.

The Seminar was made possible by a number of most generous contributions from many sources, and we would like to draw special attention to the assistance the Seminar received from the Foreign Office and Commonwealth Relations Office, and the Congress for Cultural Freedom. And finally, for the detailed organization of the event, our gratitude goes to Richard Harmston, Secretary-General of ISMUN, in Geneva; Miss Gill Walker, General Secretary of UNSA in London; and Lawrence Cockcroft and Graham de Freitas, in Cambridge.

The significance of the event was indicated by the reception of a message from the Secretary-General of the United Nations, U Thant; and we were most honoured to have with us Mr. Sture Linner, Director of the UN Information Centre, London, to read the message at the opening of the Seminar.

The value and importance of the Seminar must be seen within the context of the benefits accruing to the participants, and the framework of UNSA and ISMUN. On both these counts, the Seminar was outstandingly successful. For the participants, a further development in their appreciation of the problems discussed; for UNSA and ISMUN, the Seminar was the most ambitious national and international event ever arranged, and it seems likely that the practice of holding Seminars on specialised aspects of international affairs is likely to continue into the future. This, of course, is only one aspect of the work of UNSA and ISMUN. Internationally linked to ISMUN—the only non-international youth organisation with members from all blocs and from all continents—UNSA is active in over 100 universities and institutions of further education, creating an informed body of student opinion actively interested in world co-operation, and clarifying and upholding the aims of the United Nations. For their success, UNSA and ISMUN depend on the loyalty to and recognition of, the principles and practice of international co-operation. Such recognition can often be secured by participating in Seminars designed to examine specific problems in some depth.

PETER TREGEAR, *London*
JOHN BURLEY, *Cambridge*

Biographical Notes on the Principal Contributors

MR. A. L. ADU: Deputy Secretary-General, Commonwealth Secretariat. Previously Director of UN Special Fund Programme in East Africa, 1964-6; Secretary-General, East African Common Services Organisation, 1962-3; Secretary to the Cabinet and Permanent Secretary, Ministry of External Affairs, Ghana, 1957-61.

M. GABRIEL D'ARBOUSSIER: Director, U.N. Institute for Training and Research; Previously Senegal Ambassador to France, and permament delegate to UNESCO, 1962; Minister of Justice, Senegal, and leader of UN Delegation, 1960.

SIR JOSEPH HUTCHINSON: Drapers Professor of Agriculture, Cambridge, since 1957; President of the British Association, 1966; Chairman, Council of Makerere College, University College of East Africa, 1953-57.

MR. F. J. PEDLER: Deputy Chairman, United Africa Co. Ltd. since 1965; Director, Unilever Ltd. since 1956; Chairman, Council of Technical Education and Training in Overseas Countries, 1962; Secretary to Commission on Higher Education in East Africa and Sudan, 1937.

MR. T. E. PEPPERCORN: Director, Dunlop Rubber Co. Ltd., and associated companies.

M. DANIEL PEPY: President, Tropical Agriculture Research Institute, Paris; Previously, Technical Adviser on Aid and Co-operation, Ministry of State, 1959-60.

ROBERT W. STEEL: John Rankin Professor of Geography, University of Liverpool, since 1957; Visiting Professor, University of Ghana, 1964.

DR. CHARLES VAN DER VAEREN: EEC Commission, Brussels, with special reference to development in associated Afro-Malagasy States; Previously Technical Assistance Adviser in Planning Department of Government of Senegal; Director, Institute of Applied Economics Dakar.

Editors

PETER TREGEAR is a lecturer at the Department of Education in Tropical Areas, University of London Institute of Education; Editor of "Teacher Education in New Countries".

JOHN BURLEY read History, and Economics, at Cambridge University, and is now working in Ministry of Planning and Economic Development, Uganda.

The Diversification of African Agriculture

PROFESSOR SIR JOSEPH HUTCHINSON

I AM always ready to talk on African agriculture if I can, because it is something on which I hold strong views, not all of which are always acceptable to other people, but which I persist in propagating when I have the opportunity.

Dr. Sen, Director of FAO has remarked that Africa needs an agricultural revolution. This is something that I have been thinking about for a considerable time, and in the course of my studies here in Cambridge I have looked at British agriculture to see what made the British agricultural revolution tick, in the hope that it might give us information on how to make a revolution tick in Africa and in other developing countries. The conclusion I have come to is that there is no such thing as an agricultural revolution; agriculture has been for the last 5000 years in a continuous state of change, and so the term revolution, which is something sudden and sharp, and of short duration, is not really applicable to the kind of change with which we are concerned. Although the state of steady and continuous change has not been enjoyed by African agriculture for so long as it has been by agriculture in this country, I want to make the point that agriculture in the African continent has at least for the past century been in a state of continuous change—if you like, of continuous revolution.

I start from the proposition that the resources devoted to agriculture comprised, until recently, the sum total of the resources of the African communities, and still are by far the largest part of their productive capacity. It is for this reason that we are greatly interested in change in agriculture and, in this sense, Africa is at an early stage in the characteristic development of a civilised community. It is the function of the revolution in agriculture to release labour for the other activities of human society and to provide, from a reduced labour force, an adequate food supply for an increased non-agricultural community. It takes two-thirds to three-quarters of the population of an African country to feed the population as a whole, whereas in the West European and American trading area 10% of the population feeds the whole at a luxurious standard. This is a measure of the extent of the changes in population structure that will have to be achieved if African countries are to follow the industrial West in their development. The object of the operation is to make available to African communities the goods and other benefits that we in the West possess.

Now let us consider how Africa has begun on the road of improvement in standard of living. All such progress depends upon the development of an exchange system between town and countryside, and it is important to notice the difference between African and Asian emerging countries in the way in which this came about. In Asia there has been exchange between Asiatic agriculture and Asiatic towns for a very long period indeed. The towns and the countryside are side by side and have been interdependent through the whole history of these ancient civilisations. In Africa, on the other hand, there were virtually no towns a century ago and such centres of human population as there were, were in fact very large agricultural villages. The products of urban industry first came to Africa from the developing industrial cities of Britain and Western Europe. Now this is a point which is worth some elaboration in the context of this Seminar, in that we are particularly concerned with relations between Africa and Europe. The industrial revolution which started in Britain and spread through Western Europe and North America put the urban population of Western Europe in a position of dominance in the world such as I think no civilization had ever enjoyed before. This dominance made possible the colonisation of Africa, the creation of colonial régimes, and the establishment of circumstances in which industrial goods could be made available to Africa for the first time. The same industrial revolution had a similar effect on Asiatic countries. If you consider the cotton trade with which I was particularly concerned in my researches for a long time, the original direction of the cotton trade between India and Britain was from India to Britain. Muslin and calico are relics of the nomenclature of Indian textiles imported into this country before the industrial revolution. The industrial revolution in this country reversed that trade and sent goods, made from cotton grown in India and other countries, from Lancashire to India. These and other imports of British industrialization into India thereby put back the industrial clock in India by a very long period. It took India 30 years of protective tariffs from about 1930 to establish a textile industry that could compete on level terms with Lancashire. This they have now achieved, and they can compete with Lancashire not only in the Indian market but in the markets of Africa also. The power of Western industrialisation was so great that not only did it establish a market for industrial goods in Africa, but it drove out the industries of India and replaced their products with imported products of industries elsewhere. British industry put India back to the state of an agricultural exporter and an industrial importer, something which was quite alien to her own civilisation.

Now the re-establishment of a satisfactory balance between town and countryside within the country has gone a long way in India. This is something which has not yet been established in Africa and which is an objective with which we shall be greatly concerned. But given the industrialization of Western Europe and the availability of goods from Western Europe, the first stage in African economic development was achieved by the development of African agriculture and not by the beginnings of industry. African agriculture was developed to provide something with which to buy the goods of the industrial West. This was the first major change in African agriculture and the traditional subsistence farming of the continent had grafted upon it an entirely new system of growing crops for export. These are known as cash crops—cash crops because the only people who had cash were the Europeans. Money had replaced cowrie shells and barter, on the basis of the money of Europe. Those who want the money of Europe have to sell something to Europeans with which to get it, and it is only useful to them when they have it, to buy European goods. Thus there was developed in Africa over the last 70 or 80 years a cash crop agriculture side by side with the traditional food crop agriculture which continued much as it was before. These cash crops were taken up in various places with great enthusiasm and enormous success, cacao in Ghana, groundnuts in the savanna belt of West Africa, cotton in East Africa and the Sudan, oil palm and robusta coffee in the forest belts and so on. It is interesting to note that only the forest belt crops were indigenous in the country. Robusta coffee and oil palm are indigenous African crops. The others were all introduced from other parts of the world. But these were the means whereby Africa achieved its first great economic advance.

Unfortunately the association of African agriculture with European industry leaves African countries continually in a weak trading position. There is a limit to the capacity of any trading area to absorb agricultural products. This has always been met by moving labour out of agriculture into other pursuits, and this can only be done within a limited geographical range of the place where the people now live. Admittedly we have absorbed many thousands of West Indians and Pakistanis and some Africans into this country. This is a part of the process, but it is no solution. The only solution is to move Africans out of African agriculture into African urban occupations. We have the same problem in this country. Our agricultural problem areas are those areas which are so far from alternative industrial opportunities that the movement does not go on fast enough to match the improvement in agricultural technology, and they have fallen behind the standards of living that other people have achieved.

So we are faced with a problem in that the demand for African agricultural products in the markets of the world is limited, the rate at which they can be produced is increasing, and we have reached a position of near saturation in the market for most African export crops. Saturation shows itself not in complete failure to dispose of crops but in wide fluctuations in price according to the size of the crop and the demand of the moment. Consequently very serious fluctuations arise in the economic position of the countries dependent upon these crops. For example, production of Sudan cotton has been greatly increased. In years when there is a coincidence of a large crop and a quite small fall in world demand for cotton for various reasons, the marketing of the Sudan crop may actually come to an end. Then they are left with a substantial carry-over for which there is no market. Usually, so far, circumstances have changed rapidly. A good crop is very often followed by a bad one and the surplus from the year before can be unloaded in the following year, particularly if the demand should rise. This leads to extreme instability in the country's finance and it may be necessary to get rid of a surplus at ruinous prices. Cacao and sisal are in a similar precarious position. When you see British farmers burning straw in East Anglia, just remember not only what that means to the bird-life in the hedgerow, but what it also means for the sisal exporters of Tanzania. If we in England no longer need to use straw Tanzania will not sell sisal to make baler twine. It has been said that the coffee market depends on Western prosperity and frost in Brazil, the former to keep up demand, and the latter to provide a check on supply. Vegetable oils were in short supply after the last war, but the predicted shortage vanished. Supplies are adequate and the market is now threatened by developments in the production and technology of soya oil in the U.S.A. These things work both ways, of course, and there are some interesting notes in a bulletin from the USDA Foreign Agricultural Services to the effect that a large crop of peanuts in French West Africa or Nigeria tends to push down prices received by United States farmers. So we are all in the same boat. Agricultural produce saleable on the world market can only be absorbed in limited quantities. I do not suggest that we have reached the limit of the export of the traditional cash crops. One of the interesting political features of recent years has been the developing relations between African countries and Russia and China. It seems to me that one of the underlying factors determining this is the possibility that Russia and China may offer markets for African cash crops which will supplement those of the West. Russia, I understand, is now the biggest buyer of Malaysian rubber. And so, it seems to me that there is everything to be said for good relations with the communist bloc as a means of increasing the volume of the exchange of African cash crops for industrial products from the north temperate regions. We can increase the export to some extent to this country. It is a matter of how much we want to do. We can increase exports of these crops, perhaps by the order of 10%, but when it can be stated that the average gross cash income of Africans in Malawi in 1958 was £22 10*s*. 0*d*. per family, an increase in 10% is not going to raise the standard of living to an amount that is going to be any way satisfactory to Malawi politicians or to the people of the country. Add 10% and we reach £25 per head. What we want to do is to multiply by 10. We are much more interested in £250 per head than in £25, and if that is what we seek the traditional (traditional in the sense of the last 50 or 60 years) exchange between cash crops grown in Africa and industrial produce of north temperate regions will not carry the economy to the next stage of development. We have to do something more.

Now I believe that it is essential to appreciate this cash crop situation before attempting to assess what contribution agriculture can be expected to make to economic growth. The free world may be ready and able to use two motor-cars where one did before, but it is not able to drink two cups of coffee or eat two bars of chocolate or consume 2 lb. of margarine where one did before. Therefore the problems of increasing agricultural productivity and increasing the contribution of agriculture to the economic life of the country are something different from the problems of increasing the contribution, let us say, of textile mills or a motor-car industry to the economy. Let us accept this, but then let us also remember that there is no escaping the fact that it is from the sale of these crops that the purchase of development goods, equipment, technical services and so on must be financed. So it seems to me evident that the hope of a real advance in Africa hangs on the ability of African communities to diversify their own activities and to become less dependent on the rest of the world for goods and services in order that there shall be enough foreign exchange to buy those things that have to come from outside.

This means urbanisation and industrialisation, and I am not concerned with that. It will be discussed by other speakers later on.

I am concerned with the market that this offers to the agricultural side, and the responsibility it lays upon the agriculturalist to be able to produce the food that this increasing urban population will require. To the farmer, urbanisation means the development of the market of food. The way in which an African farmer responds to such an opportunity can be seen in the countryside within reach of any African city. For 15 miles round Kampala, for instance, milk is produced and taken in on bicycles into the town. This is an old English pattern of dairy farming close to the town. The man who produces the milk, either himself or through a friend or a relative or a son, carrys out the retailing from, in England a horse and cart, in Africa a bicycle. He has his regular clientele, his regular supply of a small amount of milk to a small number of people. Over a much wider area, a radius of 60 or 70 miles, a day's journey by lorry, the main foodstuffs of the town are brought in, and the food crop agriculture of the major town supply area is among the most advanced in the territory. Similarly, within range of Nairobi, Kikuyu farmers have gone into the horticulture business. Not only lettuces and cabbages and so on, but flowers. Making a living out of the sale of flowers in Nairobi is an example of the way in which a town market can stimulate agricultural development. Now in feeding a town, bulk is fairly easily catered for and in the first instance it is bulk and cheapness that new towns demand. Town wages do not run to fancy diets, at least not in Africa, but urban life involves giving up many unconsidered trifles that collectively amounted to an important dietary supplement. Thus quality in town diets becomes a pressing problem. Here again, this is something we as communities have all experienced. The industrial revolution in this country resulted in a substantial reduction in the standard of diet of the new town dwellers. Town wages meant poor diets because townsmen could only afford to buy the cheap bulky foods that came into the town. Moreover, they did not realise that they, and particularly their children, depended a great deal upon spinaches, fruits, berries, the odds and ends of a countryman's diet that a townsman just does not have, that a countryman does not pay for, does not even grow. They are the unconsidered extras of the wastes and hedgerows, and we have only in recent years realised their fundamental importance in good nutrition. African countrymen very often suffer from malnutrition, but African townsmen suffer more.

Ignorance is the first cause of malnutrition, low town wages and the absence of an organized supply system is the second, and there is a third factor in the town life which greatly affects African agriculture. Food habits have to change and it is worth while considering the sandwich as a symbol of urbanisation. Most simple countries, most countries in which agriculture and the community are closely integrated, live on meals which are prepared and eaten straight away. They do not keep, they are not meant to keep. They are cooked and eaten and what is not eaten then is sometimes cooked up again, but is very often thrown away. Now in a town population, there are people who work in offices and factories and so on, who are away from breakfast time to supper time and they need to eat something in the middle of the day. For this, one needs a different kind of food, something that can be cooked and kept for a day or two, something that can be prepared in the morning and taken to the office and eaten there as a midday meal without the time and trouble, and the presence of the wife to do the cooking. And so the sandwich, and wheaten flour and bully-beef have increasingly become the means whereby the African townsmen have met the problems of their new dietary situation. Wheat imports into East Africa in 1958 were 30,000 tons. This is an area which produces wheat substantially, but 30% of the requirements of East Africa were imported from Australia and the Argentine. This wheat was paid for by agricultural exports and in so far as foreign exchange is used for this sort of purpose, it is not available for the import of necessary development goods. In view of the limited capacity of the West to absorb greater quantities of the export crops of the tropics, and of the urgent need to raise living standards in the tropics by substantial amounts, I believe we need to evaluate agricultural policy with a view to seeing to it that Africa does not depend upon other agricultural countries for agricultural produce that can be provided at home.

The maintenance and modest increase of traditional exports is vital to the stability of the economy in the face of this enormous demand for development goods. Beyond that the campaign for agricultural improvement should now be directed to the food crop sector of the economy. Now the demand for food, in the economists' terms, is very inelastic, and the supply of traditional food is very elastic. In most years there is abundance and the demands of the expanding towns are easily met. Occasionally, however, there is a bad year and a town famine. This is one of the consequences of advance in Africa. Famine used to be something that happened in a bad season all over the country. Nowadays, a bad season means a famine in the town. It does not often mean a famine in the country-side. In fact, Africa has got to where Britain was in about the last decade of the eighteenth century, when a bad harvest meant food riots in the town the following April and May, because the country-man, who normally grows his own food and sells the surplus, in a bad season grows his own food and has no surplus to sell, and so it is the town that suffers. This country became secure from town famines when food imports began and there were agricultural surpluses in the rest of the world which we could buy. I sometimes quote a little note in a report of the Ministry of Agriculture a few years ago when the potato crop in this country was short. The Ministry noted that it was necessary to import 400,000 tons of ware potatoes to make up the deficiency. I contend that there ought to have been a footnote to that statement: 'Thank God somebody had 400,000 tons they did not want'. We need to remember that Britain's security in food supply has for 150 years depended upon somebody else's agricultural surplus. We have never had an agricultural surplus and have not had to bother about it. We let the Americans worry about that. But Africa needs, now that she is developing big towns, to take this into account; Africa needs to bear in mind that seasons fluctuate enormously and there must always be enough. Now a peasant subsistence agriculture learnt that lesson a long time ago, and any competent subsistence farmer always budgets for a surplus. He always grows so much that he cannot eat it all, except in a bad year. In a good year he makes beer out of what he cannot eat, and what he cannot drink he will give away, or he will cheerfully allow to rot. And that is the proper thing to do with the surplus. Of course, when towns began to develop the surplus went into the towns, and the towns were well satisfied until the year for which the peasants had been budgeting came along, and there was nothing left to go into the towns. Dr. Phyllis Dean of Cambridge University, talking about the economics of East Africa on one occasion, remarked with implicit disapproval that 10% of Tanzania's income goes in beer. I contend that this is what it was for. This was the surplus in a good year and when the season was good and there was a surplus, beer was the best thing to do with it. And as African agriculture develops to feed African towns, the first thing we have to remember is that we ought also always to plan for a surplus, because a town famine is a painful way of stimulating demand and redressing the balance between the town community and the countryside's ability to feed it.

These are the kinds of problems that face an agriculture, now for the first time with the challenge and the opportunity of an urban market. Now one further factor of major importance is involved in this problem, and that is that in the areas where there is a round-the-year rainfall the storage of food is difficult. The need to store on subsistence holdings is very slight. Cropping is so organised that there is something in the garden to dig up for every meal in the year. So the subsistence farmer does not store, he grows sweet potatoes and cassava, green bananas, beans and groundnuts and uses them as they come along. No one has ever yet built an urban civilization on the basis of a perishable food supply. A reliable supply of perishables is possible in the countryside, but it will not serve for a large town. There must be a basic storable food supply with which to meet the need in those years when the peasant farmer has no surplus to bring into the towns. And this again, calls for changes in agricultural practice.

So the townsman needs a storable basic food supply, foods that lend themselves to town eating habits, a range of foods that will provide a balanced diet and at least the beginnings of a high-value luxury diet. And it is to the supply of these needs that agricultural policy and research should now be directed, if I am right that the development of the higher standard of living in African countries can only come by a division of labour among African people themselves, rather than by a dependence upon continued imports from outside. Storage means essentially that grain is used instead of roots and green vegetables. In those countries which depend upon roots and green vegetables there is usually no difficulty, except that it is necessary to have drying equipment, which is now standard practice in temperate countries. Foods planned for town eating call primarily for imaginative cooking investigations. We go to bread and bully beef because that is what townsmen in other parts of the world eat, but there is no reason why we should not set out to do something serious about maize flour, groundnuts, beans and so on. Let us devise new methods of cooking these foodstuffs to provide the essence of a town diet, so as to provide meals that can be taken out and eaten some hours after they are cooked. This seems to me to be something of very high priority if the contribution of agriculture to the foreign exchange situation is to be maintained at its highest level. If agricultural exports are to be used to buy capital goods that cannot possibly be produced at home, then farming and food preparation must be so organised that it is not necessary to import essential foods for town use.

Many of the products needed for a good town diet are very readily produced in African circumstances, but little has been done on animal husbandry, the development of dairy products and the meat industry. Investigations on how to improve the productivity of livestock industries have been very small indeed. The whole interest of agricultural development has been centred upon the improvement of the cash crops. I would suggest that the time has now come for a radical redeployment of agricultural research, extension work, education, agricultural policy in general, to put the weight on the improvement in the provision of adequate diets for urban use.

Now consider the prospects of this kind of development. Sudan, of the countries I know, is the one most at risk from the cash-crop problem because it has only one, cotton. They have gone in more seriously than other African countries for a policy of import substitution in the agricultural system. They have gone into sugar cane, expensively too, but they will get over that. They have set out seriously to grow their own rice (not a very large amount, but to save the cost of importing 60,000 tons of rice a year is worth while in a country with the foreign-exchange difficulties that Sudan has to cope with), and they have made up their minds that they are going to produce wheat for their own use. This is admittedly expensive and, if there were unlimited foreign exchange, quite unjustifiable. But in conditions where foreign exchange is the major limitation to industrial development, to ask the community to pay a high price if they want to eat wheaten bread and rice and sugar is a justifiable demand in the interests of economic policy.

Sudan has also developed an interest in mixed farming to increase the supply of meat. And here we come to something again on which I have strong views and with which not everybody would agree. In this country we are moving away from mixed farming. We are becoming specialists, one-enterprise farms, with crops only or stock only, and we believe that we can do it. We have fertilisers and we do not need the manure. What we do not know is whether we could ever have got our soil to this stage of fertility if we had not gone through the mixed farming stage. And what we do know is that getting the soil to a higher level of fertility can be done most cheaply by a mixed farming system with the conservation of organic manures and their return to the land. Accordingly, for countries that want on the one hand to raise the fertility of their soils to advance from the exploitive into the conservative husbandry, and on to a rising cycle of productivity in their land, and on the other hand want meat, milk and other dairy produce for the purpose of improving the quality of their town diet, mixed farming has an enormous amount to offer. This is something that Africa has hardly yet begun to practice. The people who keep cattle are usually not the people who grow crops. And it is only in places such as Kenya where they had the example before them of British mixed farming that Africans have seen what can be done in that way and have gone away and set about beginning to do it themselves. This is not to say that specialist farming does not have a place. Sudan, again, has gone in for a specialist one-crop production in what they call the 'rainlands', the 25-inch rainfall belt where there is nothing to drink in the dry weather and where in consequence nobody lives. Tractors do not have to drink in the dry weather when not in use, and it is possible to develop this country and to go in for a form of prairie farming exactly like prairie farming in Canada, except that they grow sorghum instead of wheat. There is no doubt that this area offers great prospects for the provision of the basic storable bulk food supplies of that country at an economic rate. It involves a limited foreign exchange investment in mechanisation but is free of the enormous costs that would be involved in providing perennial water supplies for other kinds of farming in that area. Just as the Canadian wheat farmer nowadays spends his winter in Florida, having drained his tractor radiator and put the thing to bed for the winter, so the Sudanese farmer drains his tractor radiator and goes off and spends the hot weather in Omdurman, returning in time to do his cultivations before the rains. He is there just for the 4 or 5 months of the cropping season. These are the kinds of things that it seems to me African farming should go in for. This is the growing contribution that African farming can make to the diversification of the African economy, the use of Africa's abundant labour to provide more of its own needs. It will require a substantial revaluation of the whole agricultural policy of the countries concerned but this is something which I think ought to be undertaken. It is only fair that agriculture should make its full contribution, and we need to decide what it is going to be, what the policy on food supplies is going to be, how to use foreign exchange to the best advantage, and how to set about diversifying, and moving some people out of agriculture to do other things in the community. We might perhaps sum it up by asking ourselves what our status symbol is going to be, a Boeing 707 or a pinta milka day.

The Agricultural Revolution in French West Africa[1]

DANIEL PEPY

WHEN one considers the fact that 80% of the population in West African countries inhabit rural areas and that the *per capita* income amounts to only fifty dollars, one readily understands why African life is fundamentally dominated by agriculture and why every Head of State has given priority in development plans to agronomic research.

I. Characteristics of the African Economy

From the technical and economic viewpoint African agriculture consists of two fundamental and distinct sectors which have little in common and are opposed on nearly every count: these are the traditional sector and the modern sector.

(a) THE TRADITIONAL SECTOR

The commodities with which this sector is concerned are mostly African in origin: millet and sorghum in the steppe and savannah regions of Senegal and the Ivory Coast; yam, palm and coconut trees in humid forest zones, especially Dahomey and Togo. Other crops, not indigenous to Africa, have invaded this sector to a considerable extent: manioc or cassava a native of Brazil, has been developed in forest regions, while rice, historically grown in Madagascar, is now spreading to many other countries.

In certain African countries, notably in the Sahelien zone because of the climatic conditions, a peasant can only work for about 40

[1] Translated from the French original.

days per year; it might be possible to redirect his energy into stock-raising but one difficulty here arises from the fact that traditional agricultural methods almost always involve a separation of these activities; even when stock-raising and arable-farming exist side by side in the same area, they are practised by different tribes.

As a consequence of this division between cultivation and stock-raising, the peasant does not employ natural fertilizers except perhaps in the western part of the Sudan where the most highly evolved peasantry in Africa is to be found. The value of organic matter as fertilizer is generally accepted there and the manure produced by small farm animals is often scattered over the fields, but this remains an isolated case and the only method widely used to enrich the soil is the bush-fire, which increases its phosphate content.

Thus agriculture, fundamentally handicapped by unfavourable climate and by soil generally poor in organic matter, is further characterised by the use of unsophisticated techniques. The only tool used in most regions is the hoe whereas animal traction would allow a man to grow about four times more than is possible using a hoe.

In these conditions, traditional agriculture gives a very low yield. In Senegal, for example in 1959, the yield per hectare was barely 900 kg.; without making a comparison with France where the yield per hectare amounts to 4 metric tons, it would seem that 2 metric tons per hectare should be reached.

The main feature of this sector from the economic point of view is that only a tiny fraction of the product is sold; the greater part is consumed by the producer.

The low growth-rate of production in this sphere has frequently been laid at the door of the former colonisers. When one sees the import figures reached in 1959 by the Mali Federation comprising Senegal and the Soudan, one understands the accuracy of these criticisms: 32,000 metric tons of millet, 135,000 metric tons of rice, 4000 metric tons of maize. These figures demonstrate the ever growing reliance on overseas sources for the countries' basic foodstuffs.

The only blue-print for agricultural development in the traditional sector has been drawn up by the Niger office whose high administrative cost had absorbed a large part of the economic benefit deriving from it.

(b) THE MODERN SECTOR

The products grown in the modern sector are only to a small extent consumed on the spot by the local population. They are destined for export markets and it was these products which engaged the attention of the former colonial powers.

Modern crops were introduced into or developed in Africa by European colonisation but in West Africa individual colonisation no longer exists (whereas in Kenya and Tanganyika expatriate settlers still possess and operate farming enterprises). The production of coffee and cocoa in the Ivory Coast, as equally in neighbouring Ghana, is wholly in the hands of African farmers. It is often carried out in small units and receives technical and commercial aid from syndicates and co-operatives.

To assess the importance of export products in the African economy, it is only necessary to quote some figures; in Senegal it is estimated that groundnut production accounts for 20% of national income. More than 90% of the exports from African countries in the franc zone are agricultural products and five products alone account for 70% of these: coffee, cocoa, timber, groundnuts and cotton. Often, indeed, agricultural effort is concentrated on a single product: groundnuts represent 90% of Senegal's exports, coffee and cocoa 75% of those of the Ivory Coast.

The predominance in modern agriculture of products intended for export has very quickly brought about internal economic imbalance and great dependence on overseas markets. The various metropolises have encouraged this exploitation of the underused potentialities of the African continent—for one thing, they did not compete with the output of the metropolis; in certain cases they even provided the basis for European industries. The promotion of groundnuts in Senegal, for example, created supplies for the French oil and soapworks.

The administering authorities have set about improving the yield and quality of these crops and ensuring regular harvesting; they have fostered their development on the technical level. It was in any case easier to encourage these products than the traditional enterprises which were dedicated to food crops; the plantations were bigger, more accessible, and better equipped as regards labour and tools.

Over a long period, specialised research bodies have been set up to promote these various products: in 1941, the Institut des Fruits et Agrumes Coloniaux (IFAC); in 1942, the Institut de Recherches pour les Huiles et les Oléagineux (IRHO); in 1946, the Institut de Recherches sur le Coton et les Textiles (IRCT); in 1957, Institut Français du Café et du Cacao (IFCC). In addition, the Office de la Recherche Scientifique et Technique (ORSTOM) was established in 1943 to concentrate on fundamental research into the physical and human environment of tropical and mediterranean regions. One should also mention the work of the Niger office, in Mali for example, on the development of cotton.

But this preponderance of export crops over foodstuffs, so firmly established in the African economy, even if it is a source of substantial income, nevertheless causes an imbalance that prevents the healthy regular overall development of national resources. The frailty of these products, in technical terms (they are very vulnerable to predators, which can destroy a whole crop) and in economic terms (because of fluctuations in world prices) is one aspect of this imbalance.

It must not be forgotten, furthermore, that the development of these products often comes about at the expense of foodstuffs. The expansion of export crops has often brought about a reduction in the acreage given over to foodstuffs. It would be difficult for the African peasant to resist the temptation of cash crops when he compares the different returns to be obtained; compared with cotton at 30,000 F.CFA for 1 metric ton per hectare, groundnuts at 30,000 F.CFA for 15,000 kg per hectare, palm oil fetching 180,000 F.CFA for the 3000 kg which 1 hectare of oil palm can produce, the average price for the raw product of 1 hectare of millet or sorghum amounts to 8000 F.CFA for a yield of 400 kg.

2. The Agricultural "Revolution"

In an effort to change the technical and economic basis of traditional agriculture in tropical countries, economists anxious to give real meaning to the aims of development have joined with politicians in newly independent states keen to provide a vehicle to satisfy the aspirations of the majority in essentially agricultural countries.

Maintaining and improving exports remains one of the aims of development plans since it is through export-sales that the states will be able to obtain the assets of equipment that they need. But the goal to be achieved has become that of giving new impetus to the production of foodstuffs. Problems of nutrition abound in Africa: famine in years of drought, or locust-swarms, for example; nutritional deficiency above all in children (kwashiorkor, underfeeding etc.)—these can only be solved when African food production reaches that of temperate countries.

(a) TECHNICAL MEANS USED TO IMPROVE AGRICULTURE

It is technically possible to improve African agriculture in different spheres; research has brought to light measures which can increase the quantity of African agricultural output in the very near future.

In the genetic field, the discovery of new strains and the processes of hybridization increases yield dramatically. For example, the yield of cotton in family owned farms in Zambia is about 300 kg per hectare, but the use of improved strains coupled with the use of manure has given yields rising to 2600 kg per hectare at the research establishment on Mount Mukulu. The increase in the yield of sorghum in Senegal, thanks to the work of IRAT varies between 12% and 60% according to the strain used.

The struggle against crop pests is another preoccupation of research workers. Plant-protection in a tropical climate is even more important than in a temperate climate. Entomologists and other specialists in the fight against crop pests must endeavour to find the cause of damage and above all the ways of dealing with it. In Senegal it was necessary to burn out the millet eater. The spectacular results achieved in combating locusts and birds are well known. Equally important results have been achieved in other fields, for example in such cases as Fidj disease which attacks sugar-cane, mosaic which destroys cassava, and blight which attacks maize (in 1950 and 1952 attacks of blight were so violent in West Africa that in some areas more than 50% of the maize crop was lost). Plant-conservation raises similar problems. Recent studies have shown that 35% of the annual maize output of Togo was being destroyed by weevils; first attempts to educate the public in this matter lead one to think that the figure could quickly drop to 10% or 15%.

The sustenance and enrichment of soil presents another problem for solution. The introduction of fertiliser has enabled the yield of millet and sorghum to be doubled or trebled on traditional farms in the Mossi regions of Upper Volta.

Equally one can quote the important research done by the newest of the specialised research institutes, the Institut de Recherches Agronomiques Tropicales et des Cultures Vivrières (IRAT) into improving the function of the soil. In the initial stage this research consists of determining soil deficiencies in the earth in which plants have been grown. It was first applied on a large scale to 144 hectares of sorghum and millet crops in Upper Volta. Restorative manure has the effect of increasing to 1892 kg per hectare and 1340 kg per hectare respectively the yield of panicles or ears of sorghum and millet whereas the average figures for these crops when grown without manure are 858 and 707 kg per hectare.

Inexpensive, easily applied techniques have been adopted for the use of water. In Upper Volta the countryside has been transformed in a few years by the building of small earth-dykes which enable water to be retained throughout the year over several hectares and thus allow the soil to be in constant use. Bigger projects are under discussion. Some may seem thoroughly utopian like that of a vast dam across the Congo which would irrigate the Sahara. But successful experiments, in desalinating water for example, give glimpses of a total transformation of present day techniques.

Finally, while it is clear that the future of African agriculture depends on mechanisation, this must, in the light of some unfortunate experiments, be pursued with caution. Knowledge of the reaction of African soil to mechanisation is incomplete. The earth is fragile and shallow; while animal traction may replace the traditional hoe to great advantage, caution must be exercised before using tractors. In the Niger, an experiment with mechanisation gave spectacular results after one year but after three the sub-soil rose to the surface and cultivation was impossible. More mechanisation should be introduced, but it should be regarded as purely experimental before such methods—whose ill-considered use might destroy the soil—become widespread.

(b) HUMAN MEANS

Nevertheless none of these technical or economic changes can be carried out without a change in men, their mental attitude, habits and education.

During the colonial era, teaching was too 'bookish' in its approach to contribute greatly to the education and progress of the peasant class in Africa. From school-entry onwards, the object must be a type of education better suited to living and working conditions in African countries.

In his book *False Start in Africa*, Professor Dumont has advocated the establishment of farm-schools in which children would receive along with theoretical knowledge to equip them for advanced study, practical instruction to prepare them for the part which they will have to play in their country's agricultural progress. That would seem to be an excellent formula for the early stages in these countries.

But at a higher level research is in need of men who have been fully educated and have done advanced specialised work. The more national the basis of research, the more effective it will be since, on the one hand, a country's scientific independence sets the seal on its political independence, while, on the other, further knowledge of the place where it will be applied and of local reaction to progressive ideas enables one to be sure that the research work undertaken will answer real needs.

An ever-increasing number of African students destined for agronomic research go on to study at French and African universities. Others, on leaving the secondary school, do a course of tropical economy at the CNEAT (Centre National d'Études Agronomiques Tropicales) at Nogent-sur-Marne; followed by a session in which they specialise in the study of the topic of greatest interest to them (genetics, pedology, fertilization, phytopathology, technology etc.)—this time at the ORSTOM laboratories at Bondy or on the staff of the various institutes of applied tropical research mentioned earlier.

Popularising and dissemmating the results of research make an even more direct impact on the development of African agriculture. In an effort to reach every producer, there is an increasing use of radio and cinema. Audio-visual methods are much more effective at informing and converting the peasant population than simply handing-out brochures, which a few years ago was the only method in existence. In order to put the results of agronomic research at the disposal of those engaged in agriculture, development corporations have been set up: the CFDT (Compagnie Française pour le Developpement du Textile), the BDPA (Bureau pour le Developpement de la Production Agricole), and SATEC (Société d'Aide Technique et de Cooperation).

The third aspect into which the human element enters consists of the organizational framework. This varies from state to state since it is closely linked with the political context. In certain countries it can be set up in much the same authoritarian manner as in a military regime. In others it functions instead through a co-operative system which gathers up African traditions and transforms them by contributing modern standards. Everywhere the prime object of the framework is the adaptation of tradition to modern conditions.

It is no longer possible to leave the solution to time and wait for the spontaneous regeneration of African agriculture. Nor can new needs be met by such means as consignments of food surpluses. These can only provide a temporary and even inappropriate solution.

The regeneration of agriculture can be attained only by way of voluntary redirection of effort within the framework of the plan:

the kind of orientation depends primarily on the type of farming. Here the requirements vary from country to country but certain problems frequently reoccur:

increasing food production,
relating breeding and cultivation,
rectifying the defects of the one crop system.

In planning, the link between agriculture and industry must also be allowed for in two ways: by establishing foodstuff industries which will convert agricultural products on the spot so that finished products will be exported in place of raw materials; in addition, local industry must be directed to the production of fertilisers and pesticides.

In these circumstances, African agriculture would appear to have a good chance of success. The main requirement is to regard both the end and the means of its growth as part of an overall picture of development and not to concentrate only on the purely technical aspects.

Discussion[1]

THE principal point of Professor Hutchinson's paper—the need to diversify agriculture—aroused wide discussion and comment. It was suggested, for example, that such a policy of diversification might well be limited either by a lack of effective demand in urban areas or by a shortfall in foreign exchange earnings or external aid required to finance diversifications. The earning of foreign exchange currency is of crucial importance in all developing countries and it was not clear how diversification would increase this supply. It was pointed out that the policy implications of diversification remained to maximise foreign exchange earnings through the export of cash crops, to maximise the production and consumption of local crops, thereby minimising foreign exchange expenditure on food imports and releasing funds for the import of capital goods. Furthermore, the growth of the market economy should stimulate the subsistence grower to move from traditional to more modern attitudes and produce a marketable surplus of food crops. The successful execution of a policy of diversification postulated a certain level of education in the farmer.

Mr. Pepy remarked that although modernisation schemes should always pay close attention to the social and technical aspects of traditional methods, the primary objective should be to make the price of the export commodity competitive in the world market. Conditions and circumstances will vary from region to region but the main purpose must always remain to increase productivity, releasing labour and capital for employment in other sectors. This required a policy of modernisation as well as diversification.

A number of points were raised on the need to stabilise the price of primary products. Internally this was felt to be the proper respon-

[1] Although Professor Hutchinson and M. Pepy addressed the Seminar on separate occasions, the discussions following their talks covered similar points and a joint report of both discussions was written (Eds.).

sibility of the government. On the world market it was noted that the Marketing Boards of, for example, Nigeria and Uganda had proved inadequate to cope with the problems of wide fluctuations in price. Although some expressed the view that the diversification of agriculture would remove the dependency on a single crop, others would prefer to proceed first with the development of industry. There was general agreement that the countries which suffer from falling prices and worsening terms of trade merit some degree of compensation while measures are taken to stabilise prices at an internationally agreed level. M. Pepy, while not minimising the political problems involved, felt that greater collaboration between the producers of primary products would offset some of the difficulties they experience.

A third major topic considered was that of the balance of investment as between industry and agriculture. It was clear that, within the available (and scarce) resources, priorities must be established. Some countries are unlikely to become industrialised. In those, such as the Sudan, agricultural diversification will have a more limited aim of conserving foreign exchange. Investment in agriculture should wherever possible look for quick returns from small capital input, e.g. in the construction of earth dykes. There was, however, agreement that it was not possible to state a clear preference between labour-intensive and labour-saving techniques. The nature of the soil and climate, the relative density of population and supply of labour, among other conditions, varied so widely that each technique needed to be adapted to suit the human and environmental factors present in the agricultural community.

Among various measures suggested to improve agricultural productivity, the Seminar considered in particular the following:

1. Improvement in transport and communications was felt to be essential, especially for transferring food from areas of surplus to areas of deficit both within a country and, where possible, within a region.
2. Fundamental research in agriculture was seen to be of prime importance and concern was expressed at the disappointingly low proportion of Africans currently engaged in research

programmes. Possibly one of the most significant contributions that the educational system could make to agricultural productivity lay in this field.

3. Each country's problems needed to be considered regionally in relation to its neighbours' difficulties and the overall potentiality of the region.
4. As regards the institutional form of organisation most likely to raise productivity it was felt that the criterion should be efficiency and not ideology, especially concerning collectivisation. A certain amount of reorganisation and regrouping of population would be necessary, and often desirable.

The Establishment of an Industrial Complex

PROFESSOR R. W. STEEL

AGRICULTURE is the basic occupation of the vast majority of the peoples of Africa and is likely to remain the main source of the food supply and the chief producer of commodities for export for the forseeable future in nearly every part of the continent. Its importance as the basis of rural development and the need for an African agricultural revolution have rightly been stressed through the establishment of the Commission on Rural Development and through the first discussions arranged for the Seminar.

Nevertheless, there are some parts of Africa with prospects for industrialisation, and these are not confined to the southern areas with their large white populations in Rhodesia and the Republic of South Africa. Industrial development not only strengthens and diversifies an economy; it can also provide employment, a particularly important function in countries where an agricultural revolution could render large numbers of workers surplus to agricultural requirements and where, already, there is a marked and growing tendency towards urbanization.

At the outset there is a need to distinguish between, first the establishment of manufacturing industries on a fairly small scale, such as is taking place on the edges or in the industrial estates of many of the towns of Africa today (e.g. food processing, brewing, textile manufacture, furniture-making, car assembling, etc.); and secondly, the establishment of industrial complexes, where large labour forces are employed, where there is some development of the heavier types of industry, and where there may be considerable integration and connection between the different industries. The first development is taking place widely but often on only a small scale, and has relatively little effect on employment statistics or on the volume of trade (though it may be the first stage in the evolution of an industrial complex). The second development—that of the industrial complex—is the particular concern of this paper.

It is commonly stated that among the many and variable factors that influence the locations and growth of industry these six are of special importance: the type of power supplies; the supply of raw materials; the nature of the communications; the supply of labour; the size of the market; and the availability of capital. The standing of Africa in respect of each of these factors must be looked at, however briefly: there will be particular reference to inter-tropical Africa, i.e. those parts of the continent whose development must be especially concerned with assistance from, and association with, Europe.

POWER

Tropical Africa is not well endowed with supplies of solid fuel, but its hydroelectric potential is tremendous and rivalled only by the possibilities of tropical Latin America. Much capital is essential for such developments (e.g. the Owen Falls Dam on Lake Victoria, Kariba on the Zambezi, the Akosombo dam on the Volta) and they must be closely related to general economic potentialities.

RAW MATERIALS

Many of these are agricultural in nature, but tropical Africa produces large quantities of minerals like copper, iron ore, manganese, and bauxite as well as industrial crops, such as sisal and rubber, and hardwood timbers. To date these have generally been exported without processing. Perhaps during the colonial period countries were not encouraged to develop internal processing and manufacturing. Are prospects better in these post-independence days? By and large tropical Africa has not been over-endowed by nature, though its production is by no means insignificant.

COMMUNICATIONS

In general these are poor and inadequate, and the provision of adequate rail and road networks is very expensive. Some of the potential industrial sites are very remote from existing communications, and particularly from the ports on the coast. Cost of transport is still a major problem in many parts of Africa, whether for imported manufactures (including fertilisers, so vital for the maintenance of agricultural productivity) or for the export of industrial goods.

LABOUR

Africa is a great area for labour mobility, and the large-scale movements of people over large distances are an indication of the concentration of the labour-demand in certain areas (such as the Witwatersrand, the Copperbelt of Zambia, southern Ghana, etc.) and of the dispersion of the more densely peopled areas (such as Rwanda-Burundi, Malawi, and parts of the interior of Western Africa). Often there is a marked lack of skilled labour and even of unskilled workers, perhaps because Africa by and large is an under-populated continent.

MARKETS

While there is considerable potential (e.g. Nigeria has, according to the latest census, 55 million inhabitants), the average standard of living (and therefore the purchasing power of the individual) is low. But newly independent countries may seek by protective legislation to retain their own internal markets for home-produced goods; if they all do this, however, they will defeat their own objectives. We might consider whether there is a possibility of the emergence of certain industrial areas for the supply of extensive markets in their own and also adjacent countries—south-eastern Ghana or Lagos–Ibadan in Nigeria for West Africa, for example, or Nairobi–Thika in Kenya or Owen Falls (Jinja) in Uganda for East Africa.

CAPITAL

This is of supreme importance, and conditions for capital-attraction and capital-accumulation need careful study. Here Europe's past could be vital—or fatal—for the emergence of a more diversified, partly industrialised, tropical African economy. Without capital, the other factors can hardly operate; yet the latter are important, because capital invested where other factors are not favourable, or are even nonexistent, cannot achieve any substantial or lasting results.

Through the operation of these factors of location, certain limited areas emerge in Africa south of the Sahara where industrial complexes have developed or might develop. South Africa—with its special conditions (and its peculiar and often overwhelming social and racial problems)—is omitted since it lies outside the tropics (this in part explains the size of its settled white population, one-third of the total population of 15 millions). The areas include the 'midlands' of Rhodesia (from Salisbury to Bulawayo); the Copperbelt of Zambia; the Jinja-Tororo districts of Uganda adjacent to the Owen Falls dam on the Nile; the Lagos and Ibadan areas of Nigeria; and the Accra–Tema–Akosombo districts of south-eastern Ghana.

So far there have been three fields of industry in which developments have occurred, or seem likely to take place, in tropical Africa. There is the processing of primary products that are otherwise exported. These include the production of oil from oil-seeds and nuts—such as palm oil, coconut oil, and groundnut oil; the refining of petroleum from crude oil; and the manufacture of alumina and aluminium from bauxite. Secondly, there are consumer-goods which do not have great economies of large-scale production and for which an internal market already exists: commodities like shoes, for example, or textile goods, furniture-manufacture, the making of soap, and food processing and canning. Thirdly, there are the assembly industries where it may not be profitable to manufacture articles but there the assembling of them together can save transport costs and also foreign exchange: car assembly and the making of bicycles are examples of this third type of industry.

South-eastern Ghana constitutes a particularly good example of the prospects and the problems of developing areas in tropical Africa. The complex of industrial development planned for the area centres upon three places: Accra, the capital, a rapidly growing city of already 450,000 people; Tema, the new and artificial port built between 1955 and 1962, for the benefit of the increasing trade of the eastern areas of Ghana and also in the hope that the Volta River Project would be realised, as in fact has been the case; and Akosombo, on the dam at the southern end of the newly created Lake Volta, where large quantities of hydroelectric power will be generated. The Project is the *raison d'etre* of most of these developments, and it is indeed the cornerstone of the Seven-Year Development Plan of Ghana designed to cover the period 1963-70.

The Project has quite a long history and antedates the independence of Ghana by many years. Bauxite was discovered in large quantities in several parts of the country over 50 years ago, and talk of the exploitation of these resources for the manufacture of aluminium began then. Between the wars a South African engineer, Mr. Duncan Rose, formulated plans for the damming of the Volta that are very close to those that have in fact been carried out recently. The Government of the Gold Coast first appeared on the scene in 1949 when it commissioned the firm of Sir William Halcrow and Partners to investigate the prospects of a Volta scheme in relation to the development of the country's general economy. The report, presented in 1951, was favourable and stated the scale of the financial commitment involved. A White Paper (Cmd. 8702) was published in 1952, followed a few months later by the establishment of a Preparatory Commission under the chairmanship of Commander (later Sir Robert) Jackson.

Leaving aside the details of the subsequent vicissitudes of the Project, the important facts are these. In 1956 the Preparatory Commission reported in three large volumes. The Gold Coast became independent, as the new state of Ghana, in the following year. Just at that moment there was a very marked fall in the world price in the demand for aluminium, so that it looked for a time as if the Project, like so many other worth-while schemes for developing countries, would have to go into abeyance and be pigeon-holed in the Government's offices. To prevent this, a new technical assessment was sought by the Government of Ghana from the Kaiser Corporation of California. The Kaiser Report, by modifying the project in certain particulars and by moving the dam site about a couple of miles downstream from Ajena to Akosombo, suggested substantial economies and satisfied all the interests concerned including the aluminium companies who combined to form VALCO —the Volta Aluminium Company Limited. The contract for the dam was awarded to the same Italian consortium, Impregilo, that had built the Kariba dam on the Zambesi, and work started in January 1961.

Today the work is complete and Lake Volta is growing steadily in size and will eventually be one of the largest man-created lakes in the world, stretching for 250 miles above the dam and having a surface area of 3275 square miles. The main dam, of rockfill type, is 2100 feet long and rises 244 feet above river level and 370 feet above the foundations. A subsidiary saddle dam is 1200 feet long and 120 feet high. The power-station will have an initial capacity of 589 megawatts in 1967 and eventually a capacity of 883 megawatts. Perhaps these figures become more meaningful if it is recognised that even the smaller figure—598 megawatts—is five times that of the installed capacity of all the electric plants in Ghana in 1961.

This figure is also the measure of the availability of power—cheap power—in a country that has not hitherto been over-endowed with fuel and power supplies and in a continent where shortage of power has undoubtedly inhibited as yet industrial development on any scale. It emphasises too that in considering the establishment of an industrial complex in Ghana we are concerned not with the typical but with the highly unusual: indeed it is almost the only example of its kind. The unusual and exceptional nature of the case is further underlined by the scale of the finance involved—£G70 million for the Volta River Authority's concerns, with a further £G60-70 million for VALCO's operations in erecting and commissioning an aluminium smelter at Tema.

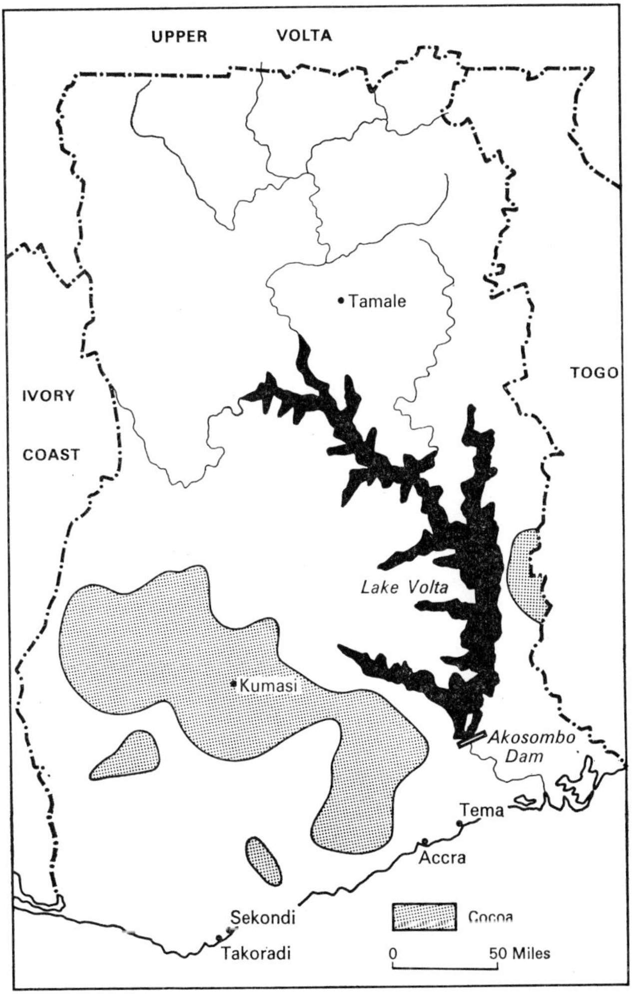

FIG. 1. The Volta River Project, Ghana.

Aluminium production is in fact the key to this development and the aspect that makes it economically viable in the long term. There are two processes in its manufacture. First, there is the recovery from bauxite of commercially pure aluminium oxide (alumina), by means of a process that involves the use of caustic soda and of energy. Secondly, alumina is reduced by electrolysis to aluminium in specially designed cells: for this, very large quantities of energy are necessary, and here lies the special importance of plenty of cheap hydroelectricity. In the early stages of the Project, alumina will be imported into Tema from Kaiser's plant in Louisiana, though later it is anticipated that Ghana's own extensive supplies of bauxite will be used and brought to Tema for alumina processing and smelting.

Aluminium, then, has justified the launching of this large, ambitious and costly programme. But in the process, cheap electricity became available for other industrial development—more than three-fifths of the country's population lives in the southern third of Ghana. Here are all the large towns—Accra, Kumasi, Takoradi and Sekondi—together with the areas where gold, manganese and diamonds are obtained and where hardwood timber is exploited in the rain-forest area. It is also the part of Ghana important for the growing of cocoa which up to now has been the basis of the country's economy. It is this economically developed third of Ghana that is likely to benefit most from the new availability of cheap electricity and where industrial prospects are greatest, in terms of both the availability of power and raw materials and the presence of the market. Already there are well-established industrial estates near all the large towns, and particularly important developments are planned for the new port of Tema. Apart from the usual port industries, there is an iron and steel works, using scrap as raw material, ship-repairing, a cocoa factory, and a variety of other food-processing industries. Tema township is growing rapidly and already has more than 40,000 inhabitants: within 10 years or so it is thought that it may merge with Accra, across the intervening 17 miles, to form part of a conurbation with a population exceeding $1\frac{1}{4}$ millions

Subsidiary aspects of the Volta Project are important: these include the eventual use of part of the water of the new lake for irrigation in the dry area of the Accra Plains; the development of navigation services on the lake itself; the provision of better water supplies; and the establishment of commercial fisheries that could make an important contribution to the improvement of the quality of food supplies in many parts of Ghana. But it is the provision of cheap electricity, and the resultant effects upon industrialisation, that is all important and gives Ghana a much better chance of diversifying its economy in this way than is the case with other newly independent African countries.

Ghana is, in fact, far from typical of tropical Africa as a whole. It is a country that has long experienced the accumulation of capital resources through the prosperity, over many years, of cocoa-farming. Two-fifths of the world's cocoa comes from Ghana, and cocoa has long been the backbone of the country's economy. Mineral production (gold, manganese, industrial diamonds and, latterly, bauxite) has also made a significant contribution to the economy, and in the last 20 years the exploitation of hardwood timber in the forest country of the south has also been of increasing importance. By and large capital has been attracted to the country—the first tropical African state to gain its independence after the war—even when the political situation might have discouraged such a flow. On the whole Ghana has had more of a tradition for economic development, and its people have had more skill and technical knowledge, than has been the case in most African countries: and with a high standard of living (compared with most parts of Africa), the purchasing power of some at least of its 7½ million inhabitants has been relatively great. Ghana has then had a chance of doing things that most African states cannot.

What we must recognise is that industrialisation is not going to happen easily or widely throughout the developing countries of Africa. It is not just a question of pumping in capital—dollars, pounds, roubles, or anything else—or even of accepting whatever technical aid and assistance are offered. There are, we must remember, many economic and social factors that inhibit industrial development, and many problems of the African environment that are the special concern of a geographer like myself. All these discourage any real development of manufacturing industry in many, if not most, countries in Africa today. We are living in a fool's paradise if we expect Africa to produce overnight a Japan, with its intensive development of both industry and agriculture, or an India with its potentially large market and very considerable supply of labour.

But this is not to discourage all industrial development except in those rare instances where all the economic conditions favour it. There may often be overwhelmingly strong social or political reasons for fostering a particular development, perhaps by protective customs or by initial governmental assistance through subsidies or tax rebate. In Britain, in what we once called our Distressed Areas, now our Special or Development Areas, we have sometimes invested capital in enterprises or areas that seemed less desirable—on purely economic grounds—than some others: this was done for the good of the people there and for the maintenance of the socio-economic fabric of the community at large. So in the countries of the Developing World external sources of capital and technical know-how may often need to be made available in order to broaden the range of an economy or to back up the reality of political freedom with some semblance of economic development. And such a policy can pay. After all, who, a hundred years ago, could have foreseen the emergence of Japan as the industrial power that she is today? Who, in the closing years of the Tsarist régime in Russia, could have anticipated the economic growth and stability of the modern U.S.S.R.? Who, as recently as 1939, could have forecast the replacement in Canada of agriculture by manufacturing industry as the major element in the country's economy? And can anyone of us confidently say what Africa will be like, politically, economically and socially, by the turn of the century?

Aid to Africa today is vital, absolutely vital. This is not solely for the welfare of developing Africa and its people and for their future progress: it is equally important for the welfare of Europe and America and in the self interest of their peoples. There is a wide gap between the 'haves' and the 'have-nots', between the wealthier and more affluent countries and those parts of the world that have been less well endowed by nature, and are often poverty-stricken and threatened with famine; this wide gap is, as often as not, widening instead of closing. We dare not let the Developing World become a festering sore and a source of disease by letting it fall too sharply behind the rest of the world, economically and therefore socially.

Perhaps at the moment industrial prospects in these countries do not appear to be very good. One swallow, we all know, does not make a summer, and one Volta Project cannot create an industrialised sub-continent. But a swallow in hand is worth two in the bush, and we very rightly note carefully all that has been achieved to date, limited though it may be in scale or in influence. We must remember too how changing is the world situation today. Politically there are all manner of tensions and uncertainties (fortunately watched over, even if not yet adequately enough, by the United Nations). Economically things are changing, often quite rapidly. New raw material supplies are tapped, new factories and plants are established, new sources of power are developed; the further production of hydroelectricity, or the extension of the use of nuclear energy for peaceful purposes, might transform in the years to come the present distribution of industrial activities in the developing countries of tropical Africa and elsewhere. Most important of all, there are the great shifts of population that must result by the turn of the century as total world population doubles, with particularly rapid increases in parts of Latin America, tropical Africa and monsoon Asia. The world of tomorrow will be very different from the world of today: and if it is to be a better and a happier world, it calls for great co-operation between the different nations and races of the world, which is an aspect of the theme of this Seminar that we need to keep constantly in mind.

The Private Investor in African Development

T. E. PEPPERCORN

1. Introduction

In dealing with this subject I propose to draw largely on the policy and experience of my own company and to say something of what has actually happened by way of illustration. And I shall speak particularly of manufacturing undertakings.

To give you the background and so that you may judge the practicality and scope of that experience I should tell you that the Dunlop Company first became interested in Africa in the nineties —in 1896 it sent a man to Cape Colony to set up business there and from this beginning our trading operations gradually spread all over Africa as vehicles on solid rubber or pneumatic tyres, on two wheels or four, began to make their contribution to the local transport.

South Africa was also the location for the first Dunlop factory in Africa. Tyre manufacture began in Durban in 1935 and this has since been followed by other Dunlop factories making conveyor and transmission belting, hose, flooring materials, foam products, sports goods, and a variety of general rubber goods.

In 1955 a rubber planting project was begun in Nigeria and this has since been followed by a tyre factory to which I shall refer in more detail later in this talk.

In 1959 with the encouragement of the Government of the Central African Federation a Dunlop tyre factory was set up in Bulawayo and by 1962 this had proved to be a viable investment to the Group, and a source of strength to the local economy. But in 1964 we were faced with the problem that the Federation had ceased to exist, a most serious situation since the factory depended on a larger market than Southern Rhodesia alone for its viability. Fortunately, the Rhodesian Company had established a reputation for the quality of its products and service to its customers, the Zambian and Malawi Governments were co-operative and exports to those territories continued at a satisfactory level, although competition increased. The next political development, the declaration of UDI on 11 November 1965 and the sanctions since imposed by the U.K. and other governments have created a problem of a more fundamental nature the outcome of which is yet to be determined.

Now I cite this merely as an example of how politics can frustrate purely commercial forecasts. When investing in a foreign country an assessment needs to be made of the degree of economic and political stability and it cannot be taken for granted that the market will be safe from changes in political or tariff area boundaries. This is one of the risks. It is not difficult to think of other areas where political developments some time in the future may upset commercial decisions which were sound enough at the time they were made.

To date there are three major Dunlop tyre factories in the African continent and in the course of time others may be justified. I hope to show you something of the processes by which such justification is determined but you will readily appreciate that because of the comparatively large size and cost of a minimum tyre production unit, the size of the market is the first consideration. It is likely to be some years before many African countries can offer the necessary potential unless they establish Customs and currency unions with each other. Unfortunately some seem to be moving in the opposite direction, for example the former British East African territories have shown a tendency to break the close links which they inherited from the colonial régime. Our interest in this part of Africa led to the opening of a Dunlop cycle tyre factory in Uganda last year. This has made good progress, but whether it will diversify into other products as we originally hoped, will depend on how far it will have continued access to the nearby markets.

The sketch I have just given you of Dunlop industrial development in Africa will, I hope, satisfy you that I can speak from a background of practical experience, obtained in African countries at various stages of political and economic development; and may I say that both the hard economic facts and the problems connected with the establishment of these enterprises were influenced surprisingly little by the form of government; they were very similar, irrespective of majority or minority rule. Nor are the problems of Africa unique, they are closely paralleled in other continents where my company operates.

2. The Host Country

An inevitable and very natural consequence following the independence of a country formerly ruled by a colonial power, whether in Africa or elsewhere, is a strong desire for economic development. Political independence invariably releases a great surge of creative endeavour and a determination to break free from economic dependence on the production of primary commodities for the more advanced industrial countries; commodities which are subject to the fluctuations of world prices and the proceeds of whose sale have to be used largely to pay for goods manufactured abroad. This is an aim second only in importance to self-government and equal to the desire for improved education, health services, communications and all the appurtenances and trappings of a modern state.

The rapid development of manufacturing industry is generally seen as the means of achieving this objective. It has political advantages as well. It is exciting, it is new; smoking chimneys, like new university buildings, hospitals, roads, are a clear demonstration of progress, there for all to see. There is a glamour about industrialisation which agricultural development lacks and which all too often is allowed to languish in consequence.

The material benefits are very real and altogether the reasons for a policy of industrialisation are many, sound and solid. It is a means of strengthening the balance of payments through substitution of goods made in the country for imports, it provides jobs for the growing population, large numbers of whom, particularly as the result of the education they now receive, will no longer be content to derive their living from subsistence agriculture; it brings with it new skills and it provides opportunities for the growing middle-class including university graduates in the form of managerial, administrative and technical positions. A prerequisite is the development of the infra-structure, the provision of light, power, water and other facilities which again create employment and add to the national wealth.

For all these reasons industrialisation has come to be an essential part of any development plan. It is generally recognised moreover that it can only be achieved by the importation of foreign capital and expertise derived not from government to government aid funds but from the private investor. Accepting these facts, not perhaps entirely palatable, the country bent on industrialisation adopts a realistic attitude, knowing full well that investment opportunities in other countries are not lacking and that the investor has to be attracted by the prospect of a fair return on the capital he puts at risk and the sort of attitude and conditions that will make this possible. It therefore adopts policies designed to make the prospect attractive. These follow a general broad pattern often expressed as incentives, some of which are of a positive kind and others no more than the removal of disincentives, and all designed to create the conditions necessary for a successful enterprise.

They include an undertaking of freedom to repatriate both capital and profits, perhaps the first essential. Then it is recognised that infant industries often require protection and that revenue duties normally applicable to imported raw materials would in many cases impose an intolerable burden on the cost of manufacture and must therefore be remitted. Direct encouragement is frequently afforded by pioneer status legislation providing exemption from taxes on profits for a specific industry over a period of years, with at times some assurance of exclusivity to the first to start in a particular industry, possibly in the form of an agreement not to grant the tax holiday to others. Then land may be offered, sometimes, though by no means always, on very favourable terms, frequently in a newly developed industrial area complete with roads, light, power, water and drainage. Another facility may be access to part of the required capital through loans from a development corporation.

It is our experience that incentives such as these are not offered lightly to all comers but that each case is examined on its merits, and in detail; the social and economic advantages, the effect on the balance of payments, the net gain to the country after offsetting such factors as the cost of imported raw materials, dividend payments, technical aid fees, remittance of savings by expatriate employees, and loss of revenue duty on finished goods that will no longer be imported, are all carefully weighed.

3. The Investor

You will, of course, understand that the scope of my talk excludes forms of social investment normally falling within the public sector, and therefore I must emphasise that I am discussing the attitude of prospective investors who are motivated by purely commercial considerations. Moreover, by investors in the context of this talk, I mean manufacturing companies and not those concerned entirely with finance.

Rightly, the development of manufacturing industry, with its need for business judgement and technical expertise, and the risks of loss if these are not wisely exercised, is regarded as a sector for private enterprise. The investor risks his own money, or more specifically the directors take the responsibility of risking their shareholders' money, on a venture which offers prospects of a suitable return. There are always uncertainties, risks of trading losses and even loss of capital are always present, the more so when operating in a new field, and the investor has to decide what rate of return is commensurate with that risk, whether the project under review will measure up to the requirements and what conditions are essential to its viability. Apart from business risks in the territory of operation, an investing company has to consider the yield it must offer its own shareholders to attract new capital and how this compares with the estimated net return from a new project after this has been successively taxed in both countries.

Clearly a great deal of investigation and study must precede decision and a manufacturing investor must have available a staff of experts in production, engineering, marketing, finance and taxation, so that a project can be fully evaluated before any major financial commitment is made.

A major objective of an international manufacturing company is profitable growth. In a changing and competitive world situation a company must grow in order to consolidate past performance and lay secure foundations for the future. Increasing the scope of its activities is one of the perennial problems of management. Whether in Africa or elsewhere, opportunities come forward in many guises and management has to be alert and well equipped to recognise and turn them to advantage.

The first requirement of a potential investor, having satisfied himself that a market is large enough to be of interest, is that he should believe that the climate is right for his purpose. Without this he is most unlikely to commit any part of his resources. By the 'right climate' I mean that certain questions must be answered to his satisfaction. For instance, does the country possess a reputation for political and economic stability? Is its political attitude western-looking, is it neutral, or does it lean towards an ideology incompatible with private enterprise? What is its attitude to existing as well as to intending foreign investors? What is the policy regarding remittances of dividends and free movement of capital? What restrictions exist on the employment of expatriate managers and technicians?

The known incentives are, of course, an indication of the climate, of whether the foreign investor is welcomed, but more complete answers have to be sought by investigation and enquiry.

Assuming the climate and the market size are felt to be right a preliminary contact has to be made with the Government, largely to obtain confirmation that the 'Welcome' sign is indeed out so far as the investor's particular business is concerned, and to gather more positive information as to the official attitude and the facilities which might be offered. It does, of course, happen at times that the first approach comes from the Government, the sequence of events varies a good deal.

More detailed negotiations need to be based on a full project study, as this will reveal a number of requirements which have to be explained to the government. What does this entail?

For a start, the Dunlop company sends out a small party of experts to make a survey of suitable factory sites and collect exact information about the availability and cost of power and water supplies, transport, labour, supporting engineering services and housing. A specialist buyer investigates the availability and prices of any indigenous raw materials and fuel, and the delivered cost of any which would have to be imported.

The market survey has to be completed in detail to show the requirements of finished products by individual categories and sizes, identifying the items needed in sufficient quantity to warrant local manufacture. This survey also establishes the prevailing selling price levels to the consumer and the various grades of trade customers. The quantity estimates are projected forward for several years in line with the expected market expansion. Any local peculiarities of service conditions and customer preference are noted.

From the market survey an estimate is made of the portion of the market which could be expected to be supplied from a local factory, reflecting the joint views of sales and production specialists. This might result in the elimination of low volume sizes and special lines which it would be uneconomic to produce. The next step is to prepare a schedule of factory equipment required to produce this output and a plan for the necessary factory, administration and storage buildings and for the necessary services. The cost of this capital expenditure is estimated in detail. Plans are made for the internal layout of the buildings and equipment, and estimates are made of the numbers of managers, technicians and workers required to operate the factory and the cost in salaries, wages, and fringe benefits.

Technical specifications are laid down for the products to be manufactured and from this information together with the volume estimates a detailed calculation is made of the requirements and cost of raw materials.

At the same time, the estimated quantity sales are evaluated to produce the sales turnover.

All this information is incorporated in a financial exercise which predicts the turnover and the profitability over several years and estimates the investment needed to finance the operation.

Before reaching its final form the study is probably reworked several times with variations in output, equipment and selling prices before it emerges as a balanced project for an efficient unit showing a sufficiently rewarding investment.

You will appreciate that a major project study involves a great deal of work by a great many people, skilled in marketing, engineering, rubber technology, production, accounting and finance, and the exercise of judgement based on knowledge and experience.

4. The Investor's Country

Looking back over the affairs of Dunlop in the overseas field over many years, it is difficult to recall any instance of conflict of economic interest between our company and our country. As a British company responsible to British shareholders but controlling large interests overseas, our decisions concerning overseas investment have inevitably been directed towards maximising the financial return to the parent company, and almost by definition, what was good for Dunlop was good for Britain. Of course we have made mistakes, but the steady growth in our overseas assets, and in our revenue from them, indicates that on balance good use has been made of our shareholders' money.

In his speech at the 1965 Annual General Meeting the Dunlop Chairman stated that in the previous 5 years the Company had invested £5 million in new money overseas but had sold in that period to countries where we have overseas manufacturing subsidiaries £35 million worth of raw materials, finished goods and machinery, quite apart from receiving £17 million in dividends and fees from those countries. You will understand that these revenues were derived from older investments as well as the new ones.

These figures were mentioned by the Chairman because of the doubts which were then being voiced about the effect on the balance of payments of investment abroad by industry. As distinct from portfolio investment by individuals or financial institutions, the overseas investment made by manufacturing industry is often largely in the form of exports of equipment and creates two-way trade in goods and services. It may indeed result in a fall in exports of the particular goods which are to be manufactured abroad but the change is often inevitable, while the importer's buying power is switched into other and probably more sophisticated requirements. Soundly conceived industrial investment is good for the investor, for the investor's country and for the host country and its consumers, and there could be no more short-sighted view than to assume that what is good for the investor must be bad for someone else.

However, governments have their problems, not the least of which is to maintain the value of their national currency by keeping external receipts and payments in balance. When a currency is under pressure controls over foreign investment are apt to be tightened and investments whose payoff is expected to be delayed for some years may fail to receive approval. Happily the United Kingdom has done little to restrict investment in the newly independent countries of the Commonwealth, lying as they do within the sterling area.

Nevertheless, it must be noted as still another of the investor's problems, to tailor his project to fit the current regulations of his own government and to state his case convincingly so that the necessary approvals will not be withheld.

5. The Negotiations

With a full project study, a firm plan, full documentation and the blessing of the appropriate minister, the prospective investor is in a position to undertake definitive negotiations with senior government officials. Naturally enough, a sympathetic awareness of national aspirations and sensitivities together with an understanding of the other side's point of view and recognition of their difficulties, can contribute most importantly to successful negotiations.

The Government, for instance, despite having given every encouragement to the scheme, may have to face up to critics who will label any facilities given to foreigners as a form of exploitation. The investor will therefore want to give every assistance in calculating just where the balance of advantage will lie in economic terms, including the net saving of foreign exchange, after buying some raw materials abroad, the servicing of foreign capital and other factors I have already mentioned. It may be necessary too, as part of the bargain, to help the Government to reject the charge of exploitation by agreeing to a form of partnership, through a share of the equity capital being held locally, either by individual investors or by government-sponsored institutions. This is against the traditions of some international concerns but others, including Dunlop, do recognise the arguments for such an arrangement and the advantages, provided that it effectively leaves the control in their hands.

The employment of local nationals is, of course, an important factor. The company should explain its policy and programme for training in the necessary skills at all levels, whilst, at the same time, making its case for the employment of the expatriates, experienced in the various managerial and technical activities, without whom the undertaking cannot succeed.

The possibility of exports is certain to be raised, but here it is not often possible to hold out hopes unless there is some specially favoured outlet in an adjacent territory or a supply of indigenous raw materials that is so cheap as to affect the cost of production very materially. It normally takes many years to achieve a level of efficiency and cost competitiveness comparable with those of the older industrial countries who often also have the added advantage of larger scale, so that the benefits will be in import saving, rather than in exporting.

Probably the most vital part of the negotiations, however, concerns the arrangements for tariff protection of the new industry. If the market is very large and the company aims to take only a fraction of it to start with the problem may not be crucial, but it may be a question that the minimum economic factory capacity is equivalent to a large part or even the whole of the market which must be assured to it since volume is vital to efficient operation and viability. Even the most efficient factory cannot monopolise its home market in the face of unrestricted imports from large, long established overseas factories often prepared to export at little or no profit. There is therefore a need for a clear understanding to be reached between the Government and the intending manufacturer as to the degree of protection which will be afforded. If the Government wants the industry it will meet the needs of the situation but it may well stipulate that selling price levels must not be raised above the previously existing level without its consent. Many will find this not unreasonable and indeed my own company would look somewhat askance at a project that relied for its viability on artifically high selling prices.

Lest a false impression may be given by the importance I have given to protection, I should perhaps affirm that isolation from competition is not part of the normal philosophy of international industrial companies. They have built up their business against powerful rivals in many fields and they are fully aware that the spur of competition has contributed to their efficiency.

Before leaving the subject of negotiations I might mention that they may extend over many months or even several years; they are never quick and it seldom pays to rush them.

6. Case Study

Having dealt with aspects of investment in Africa in fairly general terms, it may be helpful to illustrate by means of an actual example and I propose to give you a sketch of our experience in Nigeria. For many years we carried on with that country a substantial export trade from the U.K. principally in car, truck and cycle tyres using U.K. based 'coast houses' as local distributors. This was one of our best export markets and one we were reluctant to lose.

With good growth prospects, however, it was a likely area for local manufacture and if we were not first in the field another major tyre company might deny the market to us completely. Accordingly, during the mid-fifties we made several surveys but without satisfying ourselves than an industrial project on the required scale would be viable.

In 1955, however, a large Dunlop scheme was initiated in the shape of a rubber plantation. This very substantial indication of our willingness to invest in Nigeria was not overlooked and one of the Regional Governments became active in urging us to put up a tyre factory. Despite this, by 1960 when full independence was granted we were not committed, but the case for a factory, though still somewhat marginal, became more attractive as the Federal Government's policy of encouraging industrialisation emerged. It recognised the need for large-scale industries which were justified only if they had access to the entire Nigerian market, to be established on a national rather than on a regional basis. At the same time, the rate of growth of road transport accelerated to a marked degree, and with it the demand for tyres. The future looked promising and on the basis of a detailed project study we entered into negotiations.

Both government policy and our own inclination indicated the need to form a local company with control in our own hands, but a substantial minority investment by Nigerian interests. It soon became clear, however, that individual Nigerian investors, other than expatriate elements, were few and unaccustomed to the idea of shareholding in industrial equities. Equally clear was the rivalry between the Regional Governments. They were prepared to support developments on a regional scale but showed little interest in the idea of a national organisation such as our project required. It was impossible to please everyone and our choice of a site on an industrial estate near Lagos pleased only the Western Region. Eventually the Northern Region gave a degree of support when we participated with others in a textile project at Kaduna, and these two Regional Governments agreed to subscribe part of the equity, as did the Federal Government and the U.K. financed development corporations. A modest subscription came in from private investors and a quotation was established on the newly created Stock Exchange.

Negotiations for the minority shareholdings were protracted and so were the discussions with the Federal Government regarding tariff protection, relief from customs duties, and pioneer status giving a tax holiday. The leasing of the factory site was unexpectedly complicated and all these essential preliminaries added at least a year to our programme.

This was not due to basic differences or unreasonable demands on either side but rather to pressure of work arising from the great number of industrial projects under consideration, a shortage of professional advisors, the fact that the civil service was being Nigerianised and just finding its feet, and a not surprising uncertainty about the interpretation of the new pioneer legislation. In the absence of precedents even minor decisions were referred to a minister.

One point which emerged was the Government's close interest in the system of distribution that we proposed to adopt. Up to that time, tyre distribution had been almost entirely in the hands of the coast houses who had the necessary finance and did an excellent job so that tyres were freely available all over the country, either from their motor-vehicle agencies or from their general trading stores. The Government, however, was understandably anxious to develop Nigerian dealers of whom there were very few, and we undertook to do this and help them learn how to run their businesses.

Fairly early on in our negotiations there was an unwelcome complication in the form of the intervention of a rival international tyre company with intentions similar to our own. Our whole project had to be reassessed on the basis of providing a much smaller proportion of the market. It was certain that there would be little saving in capital cost in providing for the smaller output, one factory could supply all that was needed more economically and more cheaply and this, of course, was demonstrated to the government though without avail. Our rival had obtained the support of the Eastern Region Government and it became evident that we should have to be content with half a cake or none at all. Unwilling to be pushed aside by a competitor and confident both of the growth of market and of our ability to fight it out successfully, we pressed on with our plans, though on a reduced scale. But the need for full protection against imports was stronger than ever and this point was stressed accordingly.

Eventually a stage was reached when the Minister of Industry, after consultation with the Prime Minister, signed a letter agreeing to the most essential points without which we would not have felt able to proceed. By October 1961 the company was formed, work on the factory site started in December 1961. A team of expatriates was selected from other units in the Dunlop Group and sent to Lagos, the factory was completed on schedule and the first tyres were made at the beginning of 1963. The period from the start of site work to production was much the same as elsewhere.

From the start our policy was, and still is, to develop and train Nigerians to fill positions at all levels but this is taking time, and it is fair to give credit for the initial progress to the unstinted efforts of the expatriates, instructors, foremen, specialists of all kinds, accountants and managers. Some of them were inclined to over-work themselves rather than take time to teach their inexperienced Nigerian helpers, but by degrees this tendency is being overcome. It is very largely the second wave of Nigerian recruits who are adapting themselves best to the needs of the organisation, some of the earlier and apparently most promising trainees having decided that their qualifications had a higher scarcity value in government service.

Apart from the normal problems of starting up in a country whose labour force lacks industrial experience, including an abnormal level of machinery breakdowns, we have suffered from the lack of engineering facilities available from outside firms. Interruptions of production have been prolonged for this reason and have also occurred frequently from power cuts.

In 1965, too, we suffered from a strike which closed the factory for a month, a strike which had little to do with pay or working conditions in our plant, but which was basically against the Government.

Some of these difficulties were worse than we had bargained for, but we are not inexperienced in pioneering new industry; our forecasts made allowance for a certain amount of teething trouble and we are not far out from these forecasts. They called for a profit in the third year of production, and this has been achieved, but it is a modest one mainly because of the strike. At the beginning of the fourth year we are experiencing a better rhythm of production and there is a spirit of confidence in the management that their efforts are paying off.

The political leaders who had been controlling the Nigerian Federation and the Regions since Independence have as you know been replaced by a military government. The long-term results from this cannot be predicted with confidence, but so far business is continuing normally and we expect that the 1966 operations will show an initial return for the investors. This is not to say that we are satisfied with the level of productivity; this year on present indications the output per man hour will be about half the average Group level and we have set realistic targets to raise this to two-thirds over the next two years. Wages rates, which have been substantially increased since we have been operating, are still lower than in most industrial countries but this in itself does not guarantee low costs.

The number employed by our Nigerian company in manufacture and distribution is now about 900, of whom 42 are expatriates. Nigerians are increasingly assuming positions of responsibility, and it is planned to reduce the number of expatriates by 25% over the next 3 years. Good progress has been made with the establishment of Nigerian dealers who handle over 20% of the car and truck tyre business and more than half the cycle tyres.

I might add that the prominent international competitor I mentioned earlier received an equal measure of encouragement from the Government. To the best of our information they have encountered similar problems and we do not feel their progress has been swifter than ours—in fact, our confidence that we could hold our own is proving well-founded.

To round off this case study, it may be interesting to enlarge on the brief reference I made earlier to the Dunlop Plantation scheme in Nigeria, which began towards the end of 1955 when Dunlop leased 21,000 acres of virgin jungle in the Eastern Region of Nigeria. Today it is a developed community of around 4000 people producing rubber for Nigeria and with a smallholders scheme run in conjunction with the Government.

To give you some idea of what had to be done to bring this about, it should be understood that to begin with no normal services were available. All goods and materials had to be brought from the port some 30 miles away by a road that was often impassable. The first requirement was a base camp. This was set up and then a works department developed to handle all civil projects. Mechanical and electrical installations were carried out by British contractors.

Today there are seven villages each with its own dispensary, canteen, market, community hall and sports field. There are two schools and a 53-bed hospital. All this is set in the rubber plantation and served by more than 40 miles of road and some 6 miles of pipeline to carry fresh water. Electricity comes from our own power-station, and there is a central factory to which all the latex is brought.

An area which was entirely unproductive now supports a thriving community and the smallholders scheme affords opportunities for development through their own efforts for still more Nigerian families; 4400 acres of the leased area have been handed back to the Government of Eastern Nigeria who are financing clearing and planting, with Dunlop providing management supervision, together with training for the smallholders. When the trees come into bearing the crop will be sold through the smallholders co-operative for processing in the Dunlop factory.

7. Conclusion

I have dealt with the aspects of industrial development in Africa mainly on a practical basis, this being the best contribution I can make, but before concluding I would like to leave with you a few thoughts of a more general nature, and firstly I shall sum up how I see the role of the individual governments in relation to this question.

Without any hesitation I will affirm my conviction that governments cannot hope to create and operate under their own management, efficient manufacturing industries, and especially not in newly developing countries. Anything they can hope to gain by retaining profits in their own Treasury will tend to be at the cost of the consumer through high prices and poor quality, for genuine profits derived from efficiency in manufacture and distribution require the attitudes and drive of private enterprise, spurred on by the profit motive.

Moreover, capital is a scarce commodity and governments should not fritter away the resources they so badly need to provide improved social facilities—schools, universities, hospitals and the infra-structure of roads, railways, harbours, power and water, without which industry cannot develop.

The job of government in this context is, therefore, to provide a favourable environment for industry and to avoid arbitrary changes in the 'rules' which might frustrate carefully planned industrial developments, and destroy confidence in others which are being considered.

If the transfer of profits to the overseas capitalist is seen as a really serious problem the best remedy is to maintain such conditions that the investor will elect to plough back a proportion of them into further expansion or diversification, and eventually put in further capital, especially in the form of new and up-to-date equipment.

Neither should governments press too far or too fast for expatriate managers and technicians to be replaced by local nationals. Their skills are a valuable asset to the country in which they work and the standards they set are a healthy challenge to the local talent. These people are not inexpensive, there is a great demand for their services elsewhere and their employers will be willing enough to replace them over a period as local substitutes prove their worth.

Finally, governments should always realise that foreign private capital is not unlimited and it will flow to wherever it will secure the best return abroad consistent with security, or else remain at home. Taxation is an important factor in comparing one prospective investment with another and home governments can veto foreign investments which do not look attractive to their own balance of payments.

Now for a few general thoughts for the investor seeking profitable employment for his capital and expertise in emergent African countries.

Let him plan his investment on such lines that it will stimulate others, especially those which will afford opportunities for local private capital and enterprise. Although sometimes tempting, it is a mistake for the powerful foreign concern to be too self-sufficient and it should rather set itself a clear objective to encourage the growth of independently owned business associates, who will sell to the concern their goods and services or buy and distribute its products, thus acquiring a lively interest in its prosperity.

Not only with business associates but with national and local government authorities the industrialist should aim to encourage self-reliance rather than step in and try to do their job for them. Some measures of company-operated welfare services for employees may be normal or even essential but an excessively paternalistic approach is not in the longer term the best way to foster an intelligent and self-reliant community.

It goes without saying that the foreign-owned industrial company should pursue a vigorous policy of training local nationals for all levels of employment and should not wait for external pressure before offering suitable advancement to successful trainees.

Further the foreign investor should shed any inhibitions he may have about admitting local interests to a share in the investment. The fear that this may handicap the management or prevent the implementation of wider Group policies can be greatly exaggerated. If there is any foundation at all for such fears, this is more than offset by the benefit of identifying local interests with the success of the enterprise. I would just qualify this statement in one way—

there can be a right time for applying the policy, and it may not necessarily be in the very early stages before the earning power of the project has been proved.

To sum up these thoughts, and indeed the whole of my talk, in one sentence: the wise investor will consider not only what he can gain from the situation but also what he can contribute, since an arrangement however skilfully negotiated, is unlikely to flourish over a long period unless it continues to be attractive to both parties.

Discussion

Much of the discussion centred on the relative importance of the private sector in the promotion of industrialisation in African countries. The view was expressed both by participants and the two speakers that, to promote an inflow of private capital, the host government must establish, and maintain, conditions favourable to the private investor. Mr. Peppercorn emphasised that, where relevant, the Dunlop Rubber Company welcomed a government agency as minority shareholder. As a matter of general principle of the relationship between governments and the private sector of industry, he considered that governments should confine their activities to no more than creating the conditions favourable to rapid industrialisation. It was felt that these activities would include the vital necessity of establishing an adequate infra-structure for development: transport, communications and social overhead capital to lay the foundation for productive investment.

Since it was maintained that the origins of capital—whether foreign or domestic—would influence the nature of the production process, Professor Steel emphasised the possibilities of channelling investment—private or public—through the intermediary of international organisations to reduce the influence that foreign capital might have on development. Mr. Peppercorn maintained that no agreement between a government and a private company is satisfactory unless it is really beneficial to both. Certain firms do not accept investment which is either very risky or which would only show low returns. The ultimate aim of a government must be to reduce its dependence on foreign capital and to rely, for equity capital, on local issues. For smaller countries where the size of the market is insufficient to encourage private foreign investment, it was recognised that the public sector would need to play a larger role in the process of industrialisation.

A number of speakers thought that, rather than confine itself to the basic activities mentioned, government should go further and actively dominate all investment in the industrial sector. The private sector should be integrated into the overall economic plan and, since essentially the interests of government and private investor were identical, a partnership in some areas would be possible.

A number of specific points were made regarding the actual mechanism of private investment. The possibility of nationalisation as a factor inhibiting investment was stressed. The compensation schemes for investors organised by the governments of the United States and of West Germany in the event of appropriation were suggested as a means of alleviating this particular problem. Where balance of payments difficulties were experienced, it was suggested that the return on the investment should be reinvested in the host country and not repatriated, though it was recognised that such a measure from the host government might inhibit future investment.

The Seminar also considered the obstacles to a more rapid development of the industrial sector. In particular, the importance of intra-African trade and co-operation was stressed. It was felt that, wherever politically and economically possible, investment should have as one of its objectives the promotion of regional trade. The possibilities for regional co-operation through the development of hydroelectric power at the Volta, Owen and Kariba dams were examples which should not be overlooked and the desirability of facilitating regional trade by a transport system running parallel to the coast was emphasised.

An adverse factor in the industrialisation process was seen clearly to be the wide fluctuation in export earnings, affecting government revenues and Plan targets. An estimate was given that the loss in export earnings in recent years—from the peak prices of the early 1950s—was greater than the total inflow of aid over the same period.

Finally, the problem of the training of skilled personnel and the Africanisation of posts held in industry by expatriates was felt to be of major importance. The training of manpower in suitable skills is a long-term process and was thought to be a fruitful field for co-operation between Europe and Africa.

Manpower and Management in the Strategy of Industrial Development

F. J. PEDLER

THE development of industry in Africa is in part a response to economic factors, and a number of industries are able to flourish with little protection or subsidy, or with none: indeed, some of them make large contributions to national revenues. I have in mind such industries as cigarettes, beer, sawmilling, veneers, plywood and blockboard, cement, soap and vegetable ghee. But many other factories have been built rather in despite of economic factors, with political support which involves heavy expense to governments and consumers.

Among the many reasons underlying this enthusiasm for industrial development is a belief that it will provide employment for large numbers of people. I fear, however, that this is not good strategy. Of course, industry does create *some* employment. A cement company with an investment of £4 million employs 583 persons. A company manufacturing aluminium utensils with an investment of £125,000 employs 104. This question of numbers employed, in relation to capital invested, was examined by Mr. Bamgbose in a paper published by the Nigerian Institute of Social and Economic Research in 1962.[1] The approximate capital per worker runs from £1200 to £7000, and I have quoted his two extreme cases. I may add that my own Company's timber and plywood venture employs about 3000, or one worker for £1600 of investment.

Now, in view of these figures, employment in industry is hardly significant as a safety valve for the problem of unemployment and

[1] Bamgbose, E. A., *Industrial Policy and Small-scale Industries in Nigeria*, NISER, March 1962.

underemployment which exists in many African countries, and which threatens to become more acute by reason of the increase in population, and by reason of the large numbers of leavers from the primary and secondary schools.

When I say that employment in industry is hardly significant as a safety valve, I do not mean to discourage any useful efforts to increase the number of employees in industry. Mr. Bamgbose, in the article to which I have referred, raises the question, 'Could not industrialisation have been pushed further with more industries on a small scale with the same amount of capital investment?' He suggests that in small-scale businesses the ratio of labour to capital is normally greater.

Mr. Reddaway, Director of the Department of Applied Economics at Cambridge University, has written an article on 'External Capital and Self-Help in Developing Countries'.[2] He argues that, in developing countries, it is capital which is scarce and expensive rather than manpower. Consequently, the emphasis in the efficiency drive should be on raising the output from a given amount of capital rather than on raising the output per man. Where machines are scarce and men are plentiful, it may well be in the national interest to do this. To take a simple example, the introduction of a second or third shift will raise the daily output from the factory, and this increase is obtained without any additional capital, by making fuller and better use of capital which already exists. By making the plant work for more hours in the day—and the same applies to making it work for more days in the year—the national income will benefit, and this will probably also be true of the profits of the proprietors. The main counterpart of the increased national income will, of course, be increased payments of wages, reflecting the increased numbers of people employed. The initial difficulties involved in organising the extra shifts—ranging from the social problems of night work to the difficulty of securing a supervisor for the extra shift, and perhaps the installation of artificial lighting—should not, Mr. Reddaway concludes, be allowed to outweigh the important benefits.

[2] Reddaway, W. B., External capital and self-help in the developing countries, *Progress*, Vol. 51, No. 286, 4/(1965-6).

I have been interested in the views of Mr. Schumacher[3] which he has summarised in the expression 'intermediate technology'. I do not think that Mr. Schumacher is opposed to the setting up in Africa of large industrial units with sophisticated machinery, but he believes that at the same time an effort ought to be made to stimulate production by simpler methods in smaller units, which can employ larger numbers of people of medium skill. He believes this would stimulate a sense of personal motivation, and that it would provide a training ground for men with ability to act as technicians and supervisors.

I am sympathetic with all these lines of thought. Of Mr. Bamgbose's line of thought I would say that a healthy economy must accommodate both large-scale and smaller industrial units; but some difficulty arises for the smaller units if the standards of employment and workers' amenities are set by law or by custom at a level which only large-scale units can afford. We shall return to consider this.

Of Mr. Reddaway's views, one can only approve: and they apply equally whether one is talking of a highly sophisticated, expensive modern plant or of a more primitive collection of machinery. There will, in fact, be more incentive for the investor to work three shifts on an expensive plant than on an inexpensive plant.

Of Mr. Schumacher's views, one must observe that the application of 'intermediate technology' is perhaps even more important and urgent in agriculture and the rural industries that go with it than in industry. Here I would remind you of that fine contribution from Sir Arthur Lewis, the West Indian economist, who produced for the Government of Ghana a report 'Industrialisation and Ghana'.[4] That report contains some valuable observations on manpower strategy. Its central theme was that the first sound step towards industrialisation ought to be sought in the improvement of productivity in agriculture. Sound industrial development, said Arthur

[3] Schumacher, E. F., *Economic Development and Poverty,* Bulletin No. 1, Intermediate Technology Devpt. Co. Spt., 1966.

[4] Lewis, A. R., *Industrialisation and the Gold Coast,* Government Printer, Accra, 1953.

Lewis, would not come unless workers in the agricultural sector produced a surplus of food supplies which would enable the urban industrial workers to be fed at reasonable cost, and consequently to be employed at wages commensurate with the standard of living in the agricultural sector.

I repeat that I am sympathetic to all these lines of thought, but I do not think that any of them is likely to lead to the employment of such numbers of people in industry that industry can be regarded as a useful safety valve for the population problem. That would be an illusion; and it would be a disservice to Africa to harbour such an illusion. The main line of strategy for increasing employment opportunities should lead rather towards agriculture and other primary production.

There are, of course, other reasons for encouraging small-scale units, besides the objective of increasing employment. There are many sovereign states in Africa, and most of them have practically no industries because they are too small as markets. If these states, within their present frontiers, are to have any industrial development, it can only come in small units. Every possible encouragement should be given to the creation of customs unions, and to the preservation of those customs unions which already exist and which are so regrettably threatened by the unneighbourly attitudes generated by independence. However, that is another matter and leads away from manpower strategy.

Industrial development in Africa has had the effect of creating an *élite* class of work people. Those employed in factories are usually remunerated at levels which are much above the general income level of the country. In addition to their income they enjoy a high standard of amenties. In some cases the employer provides housing. For instance, the housing provided by the East African Tobacco Company (a subsidiary of the British-American Tobacco Company) for its workers in Nairobi was of a standard previously unimagined for workers of that income level in that part of the world. I am reminded of an incident which occurred at the opening of the soap factory in Tema in Ghana in August 1963. Dr. Kwame Nkrumah did us the honour of performing the opening ceremony. In view of certain attempts against his life, his security service had laid down the route which we should follow in conducting him round the factory and had insisted that he must not deviate from that route. At a certain point I therefore asked him to glance down to a far corner of the site in which, I said, we had provided a hospital. The President expressed great interest and immediately plunged off the route and walked the quarter of a mile which was required to see the hospital —to the great alarm of the security squad. More recently I visited my company's new brewery at Moundou on the River Logone in the Republic of Chad. The cloakrooms and washing facilities in that factory, the clothing provided for the workers and the laundry arrangements for keeping it clean, are equal to anything in the world.

Now it is quite obvious that a policy of promoting small-scale industries will involve discarding this policy of high amenities, since it is not to be imagined that small units can afford this kind of thing.

Furthermore, Mr. Reddaway's emphasis on spreading out capital which he alleges to be scarce would lead in the same direction. When you build a factory in Africa now, the costs of the canteen, the cloakroom, the washing facilities, the hospital, the laundry, the bicycle sheds and in some cases the houses, constitute a high proportion of the capital committed. Capital could be spread further by suppressing these amenities, but I am not at all sure that African governments and trade unions will willingly accept such a proposition. It would imply quite a new attitude at the International Labour Organisation.

I have referred to canteens. Factory canteens raise a special problem. They are expensive to build and to run. Of course they have to be subsidised, although it is general practice that the workers should pay the cost of the food. All factory managements are aware of the danger of paternalism and it is usual to arrange for committees to be elected by the workers and to leave the actual running of the canteen in the hands of the committee. Notwithstanding all this, in all the factory canteens with which I am acquainted, the percentage of workers who take advantage of the meals is disappointingly low. Many workers prefer to get their lunch outside the factory gate from a cook woman on credit rather than buy the subsidised meal in the canteen for cash. In these circumstances one cannot help wondering whether it would not be economically desirable, and more in accordance with the wishes of the workers, if factory canteens were suppressed.

Nearly every African who earns a good salary or a good wage is under pressure from relatives, often distant relatives, to take them into his household or give them help in some other way. Where the wage earner succumbs to these pressures, his standard of living is pulled down to the subsistence levels of remote farms, in spite of his high wage. Only the amenities are left for him to enjoy. However, it would be unwise to exaggerate this point. It is, perhaps, a greater danger for the labourers than for the more sophisticated workers who are trained in skills or who come up to the supervisor level. Among these people there is plenty of evidence of the type of spending that we associate with the affluent society.

Here in the West there is a tendency to assume that the cost of labour in Africa is low. When incomes in Africa are compared with incomes in America, they do look low. But when you compare the cost of labour in Africa with labour in Eastern countries, you can only conclude that the cost of labour in Africa is high. According to the annual statistical *Year Book* of the International Labour Office the wages of unskilled labour in Africa are just about twice the wages of unskilled labour in India: that is to say, the highest levels in Africa at places like Accra and Dakar are about twice the highest levels in India which are in Bombay, and the lowest levels in Africa in places like Bornu or the Upper Volta are about twice the lowest levels in India, which I believe are to be found in Madras. I have no statistics which enable me to compare the wages of semi-skilled and skilled labour in Africa with those prevailing in the Far East, but I am sure that the ratio is far higher than two to one. For men with any kind of craft or mechanical skill in Africa, we begin to think in terms of £7 to £10 a week and for factory supervisors we have to go up to £20 a week. At these levels African labour commands the same prices as in some European countries. And, of course, the cost of labour is greater than the salary because of the social amenities that have to be provided.

The strategy of high wages, and the strategy of maximising the numbers employed in industry, cannot live together. African governments will have to choose the one or the other. Investors have to take government policy as a datum and, as things stand, the datum is high wages and expensive amenities. To an investor who has to accept high wages and social amenities, the road to success must nearly always lead towards the use of advanced mechanical techniques. In my experience, the successful industries in Africa have been those which have faced this fact with all its implications. My own company has been successful with plywood and veneers and our plywood factories must contain the most sophisticated and advanced collection of gadgets between Dakar and Dar es Salaam.

We may also claim some success with our breweries. Here, we ventured upon an entirely new technique of brewing—the first brewery which transferred all its liquids along horizontal pipes by the use of electric pumps. This was at Kumasi in Ghana. Such factories create wealth. They are good for the countries where they are established. For the consumer they provide high-quality products at reasonable prices; for the government, a big share of the profits in the form of taxes, both direct and indirect; for a limited number of workers, high wages and good amenities; for the investors, good profits of which a considerable share can be ploughed back.

There must be a danger, if African countries follow the strategy of using old-fashioned methods—the strategy of adopting technology which is defined as 'intermediate'—that they will land themselves with inefficient producing units, and will be unable to compete in the modern world. This, of course, is particularly important in relation to export industries.

I have referred to the creation of an *élite* of industrial workers. It is indeed an *élite* because of the rigorous standards of selection which are now generally adopted by employers. In places such as Nairobi, Port Harcourt, Onitsha and Lagos there are many applicants for every job that is vacant. Employers are therefore in a position to insist upon a rigorous medical examination and it has become common practice to require applicants to undergo aptitude tests. The result is that factories in Africa can now start with a very high quality of human material—healthy, intelligent and keen. This is being reflected more and more in standards of performance. In spite of the dreadful things which used to be said about the performance of African labour, I have never doubted that Africans were capable of good performance. As long ago as 1951, when I wrote a little book about West Africa for the Methuen Home Study series, I drew attention to examples of African workers who showed cheerfulness, speed and outstanding physical performance, and I also ventured to suggest that low productivity could be traced mainly to faults of management. There has recently been much interest in this vital question of the productivity of labour. We are indebted to the Nigerian Institute of Social and Economic Research for some valuable studies relating to this question.

Wells and Warmington[5] devote a chapter to the Sapele timber industry. It may be described as an analysis of the analysers, because it shows how the managers of African Timber and Plywood Ltd. at Sapele have analysed the tasks performed by the labour and how they have adapted the system of job classification, remuneration and training to improve the efficiency of the labour.

Mr. Bispham[6] says: 'If management continues to employ and tolerate labour which is too damn lazy, then one may suspect that management is as inefficient as the worker is alleged to be'. He takes the view that, under good management, labour in Nigeria can perform satisfactorily. I am interested to find that he quotes in support of this opinion the experience of the cement works at Ewekoro. This is a firm in which the United Africa Company undertakes the commercial management. Our technical partners are Associated Portland Cement, and it is a pleasure to read Mr. Bispham's observation that the productivity of workers in that factory was exactly equal to that of their United Kingdom counterparts.

On my previous visit to Africa I had had the pleasure of seeing a workshop where radio sets were being assembled—a small-scale

[5] Wells, F. A. and Warmington, W. A., *Studies in Industrialisation—Nigeria and the Cameroon*, NISER, 1962.

[6] Bispham, W. M. L., *The Concept and Measurement of Labour Commitment and its Relevance to Nigerian Development*, NISER, 1964

industry, this, though allied to a large organisation of British manufacturers who have set up assembly plants in twenty overseas countries. After 3 months of training, every woman on the assembly line was able to solder connections at speed with either hand. Their rate of production, and the percentage of sets which were successful at the first test after coming off the assembly line, was equal to anything achieved in the twenty overseas countries.

At a soap factory in Ghana, it was decided to put the women packers on an incentive bonus, but the mistake was made of adopting norms of performance before effective tests had been conducted. The result was that the women quickly earned quite remarkable wages. One could go on multiplying instances of this kind. There is not the slightest doubt that industry in Africa, provided it uses its opportunity to make a rigorous selection of the best candidates, can depend on its workers to put up a very satisfactory performance.

I have referred to the employment of women in industry. You may have noticed a report in *The Times* on 10 March 1966 that a group of young Algerian women stalked out of a meeting in Algiers when Colonel Boumedienne, the Prime Minister, suggested to a predominantly feminine audience that men should have priority over women in the allocation of jobs. This, he said, was necessary because of heavy unemployment in Algeria. South of the Sahara there is a good deal of prejudice against the employment of women. In Tropical Africa the question raises some ticklish points. It is by no means true in all African societies that the man is responsible for the upkeep of his wife or wives and children. But, in any case, from the employer's point of view the question links up with that to which I have referred earlier, namely whether we are to employ an *élite* of labour at high levels of wages and amenities, or whether we are to take larger numbers of less expert labour—in which case the policy of high wage levels and amenities ought to be reconsidered. If it is left to us to decide whom we want to employ on soap-packing lines or on soldering radio sets, we shall continue to train and employ women.

I now move on to another problem of manpower strategy which I may sum up in the phrase 'level of skill'. The demand in industry for qualified chartered engineers with university degrees is small. In my own company's packaging plant at Apapa, which is a large operation, we employ one mechanical engineer of that kind. We have work in the factory from time to time for an electrical engineer of the highest order, but could not afford to employ one full-time so we try to make arrangements to draw on other resources within the Group.

At a plywood plant, with its high degree of sophistication, we might need as many as six or eight chartered engineers. But in all these the number of competent foremen required is numerous. I am thinking of the man with the kind of skill represented by the Higher National Certificate or Higher National Diploma. We need eight or twelve such people for every one chartered engineer. But in some African countries the educational system seems likely in the next few years to produce more university graduate engineers than Higher National Diploma supervisors. As manpower strategy such an education system is out of gear. It has, of course, been evolved in response to a tremendous demand for prestige education and it represents a concession to the African's determination to be content with nothing less than the best. However, when in a year or two the engineering faculties at Zaria and Lagos are in full production, engineering graduates will inevitably find that the opportunities open to them are mainly in the foreman and supervisor class, and not at the level of the chartered engineer. It would be good educational strategy in the manpower field to improve and extend facilities for training technicians, even if it had to be at the sacrifice of the education of engineers at university level.

I now come to questions concerning management. I think we can now, in 1966, deal with this matter without bringing in any discussion of the relative positions of African and expatriate managers. Africans hold management positions at all levels, including the top. The government immigration authorities in some countries occasionally niggle at the immigration quotas of some employers. As strategy, it would probably be better for African development if employers were allowed to decide for themselves how many expatriate managers they need: as, indeed, in some African countries they are allowed.

A more serious problem is the unneighbourliness of Africans towards one another. The displacement of the Ibo from other parts of Nigeria causes serious difficulties. The sudden reversal by President Houphouet-Boigny of his agreement with Upper Volta, Niger and Dahomey on common citizenship was both a surprise and a disappointment. But it shows the strength of feeling in Ivory Coast against foreign Africans. You will remember that in 1959 all the Togolanders and Dahomeans holding senior positions in the Ivory Coast were driven out in circumstances of painful distress. We have seen the Gabonese chased out of Congo-Brazzaville and vice versa; the Senegalese and Malians expelled from each other's countries; a number of Ghanaians and Nigerians deprived of their jobs in Congo-Leopoldville. Most tragic of all was the shooting by the Congo rebels of senior Africans in the towns which they occupied.

Every one of these actions has set back development. The free movement of management skills throughout the continent is much to be recommended. Efficient management is vital. Its importance has been sadly underrated by some African governments: those which have fallen prey to the sales talk of the factory-sellers, from both sides of the Iron Curtain. The evidence of this is seen in a number of factories in Africa which either do not operate at all, or operate at a heavy loss. It should be basic strategy that, whenever a factory is built, the management is assured before construction begins, and is thoroughly identified with the plans and the profitability. This is ideally secured by entrusting factories to equity investors: but if governments feel that they must be the owners, then they should at least fortify themselves with management contracts.

Whenever you are a manager, whether in Africa or in Europe, the first thing you have to do is to understand human beings and how to get the best out of the staff. Wherever you are, you have to understand how to use capital. You are always engaged in the struggle to keep costs down; to see that the return from the business meets all the expenses and leaves over some surplus to remunerate the capital and to finance expansion. Some managers will be working in government corporations and others will be working in private firms. Fundamentally from the manager's point of view I do not think this makes a great deal of difference. One of the services which an Institute of Management can perform is to provide a forum and a meeting-place for managers from these two main branches of the economic organisation of the country. There is now a lively Institute of Management in Nigeria and I hope we shall see similar organisations in other African countries.

Good management has to aim at creating the conception of the company or of the corporation as a community of men united for a common purpose. Managers and workpeople sometimes tend to develop different points of view, but both sides should remember at all times that they earn their living from the prosperity of the enterprise.

Of course, staff management involves dealing with trade unions, and this is one of the major questions for the modern manager. Some African unions have highly competent leadership. On the other hand, we have also seen unions whose leaders put forward demands which appear to be ludicrous. There are cases on record where demands have been made for wages to be doubled, for non-contributory pensions at the age of 50 irrespective of length of service, and for astonishing periods of annual leave. The formulation of such demands tends to provoke managers into saying they will not meet union representatives or enter into any discussions. This, however, does not appear to me to be a sound attitude for management. Although demands may sometimes seem to be irresponsible, they constitute a warning that managers have a big job of public relations to do with their own employees.

Managers should be bold and sympathetic in recognising unions and in helping them to develop along the right lines. There is need for the leading employers who have experience of this problem in many countries to lead the smaller employers, some of whom tend to see in trade unionism nothing but danger and subversion. It must, however, be admitted that there are limits beyond which a management cannot go in recognising a trade union. The important thing is that we should be willing to recognise trade unions which represent our workers. If we are pressed to recognise a union which, we know, does not represent our workers difficult problems arise. Then, of course, there is the awkward situation when there are two unions, each claiming to represent the same workers. At the extreme limit, managers may have to deal with a situation in which a trade union is organising violence to force the workers to comply with its instructions. It cannot, therefore, be said that in every case managers must recognise every trade union that presents itself but, as a general rule, we should not boggle at dealing with unions which represent our workers.

The question 'To whom does management owe responsibility?' is much discussed these days, and rightly so. The corps of managers in the great corporations and companies begins to look like a new aristocracy, a privileged class, a social order wielding great power: and the possession of power always arouses suspicion in others. 'Power corrupts', they say. It is right and proper that men should ask of us to whom we are responsible and for what. The law has much to say which is relevant: but the law lays down a minimum standard of conduct only. We operate in a climate of opinion which expects more from us than the law. A corporation or company would have dreadful public relations if it acted on the basis that it had no responsibility to the staff and their families beyond those which the law specifically imposes. And beyond the staff there is society at large. Are the corporations and companies expected to be the financial sponsors of every good cause—philanthropic, educational and artistic? Or do their responsibilities in such matters cease when they have duly paid their taxes? Of course, it should be easy to gain good-will by giving things away, being generous to staff, munificent to every public appeal, relieving the unfortunate and succouring the needy. Many members of the public will tell us that is what is expected of us. But all these fine things, if they are to be done at all, can only be done out of profits. A manager's first responsibility is to make those profits; to keep his business in economic health. This involves a constant battle against costs. Costs must be kept down to the figure which the business can afford; and that means what the customer will pay. This is the economic basis of business and it applies equally to public corporations and to private companies.

The profit and loss account is critical for every concern. A public concern which runs at a loss may be able to continue, but it can hardly hope to avoid the embarrassment of being attacked for sponging on the community. A private company which runs at a loss must go bankrupt and close, causing great distress to its staff and shareholders. Can one say, therefore, that the first responsibility of a manager to society no less than to his own board is to make the best economic use of the resources entrusted to him; to make labour and capital work together so as to produce the best value for the customers? Here we find the point of synthesis where responsibility to society and responsibility to the board of the operating unit become one and the same. In fact, it comes down to this simple glimpse of the obvious: that the responsibility of a manager is to manage.

In this matter of efficiency competition is the great spur to effort. Competition is ensured by giving customers freedom of choice between different suppliers. Managers of a company or of a corporation which works in direct competition with others are subject to a rigorous discipline. The customer has free choice between their products, their services and those supplied by competitors. On the other hand, corporations or companies which enjoy monopoly conditions are not subject to the same rigorous and automatic economic discipline. In such conditions, managers must invent and impose their own disciplines: if they do not, they can hardly complain if the public criticises and the government imposes controls.

Nigeria is perhaps unique among African countries, in that manufacturing business is becoming more competitive. In industries such as brewing, cement, weaving, textile printing, plastics, tyres, cosmetics and many others, there is already keen competition and there is reason to believe that these conditions will become more general.

Managers ought to welcome the discipline, the stimulation, of competition. We must admit that many of us, no less in the private sector than in the government sector, have sought after conditions which, if not amounting to monopoly, at all events involve protection against competition under government legislation. That is the whole sense of the Pioneer Industry legislation, and there may be good arguments why infant industries should enjoy special protection against competition for a period. It naturally comes as a shock when that period is at an end and managers have to face the full blast of competition; but this is what we must do. Nigeria herself is in competition with the rest of the world. Her exports must compete, in price and quality, on the world market. Therefore, her own internal economy must operate on a basis of costs and prices which are related to world levels. This is what competition will produce. Nigeria is indeed fortunate in being a country big enough to be able to afford to have competitive industry. Basic strategy for other African countries should be to create conditions in which management can be subjected to the discipline of competition and consumers can be blessed with its benefits.

Discussion

The question of wage rates was the first aspect to be discussed. For the United Africa Company the wage scale is different in each country where the company operates: the company follows the level of wages prevailing in each country. At higher levels of skill, the use of a job-grading system suggests that the skilled worker commands a higher wage than workers at similar levels in Europe. In the top executive positions, the local manager is able, on occasions, to attract a higher wage than the expatriate, since that wage-level is often set by competition between various other forms of employment—for example, government service, or the directorship of a public corporation.

In considering the question of the size of industrial units and the criteria of economic efficiency, Mr. Pedler maintained that a policy of high wages and high amenity costs stimulated the growth, or introduction, of large-scale industry. Sometimes, however, even the minimum economic size could be greater than the resources and market of the country could offer. It was apparent that the chief problem in manpower was not the employment of the unskilled migrant worker but the role and place in industry of the semi-educated.

Mr. Pedler's remarks on the role of trade unions raised many comments. It was felt that the diversification of the activities of the United Africa Company in Nigeria, for example, made it impossible for the management to consider union demands on a 'group wide' or 'house' basis since this would cut across the determination of wages by industry. Although it was accepted that 'house unions' decentralise the trade union movement and thus weakens its cohesion, it was thought to be inevitable at the present stage of development. One view was forcibly expressed that it was wrong to view the role of African unions from experience of European unions and that unions should not be prevented from becoming arms of political parties. On the other hand, it was argued that the production of a company should not suffer by reason of political factors in which the company had played no part. Unions were more likely to achieve more for their members if they concentrated on the problems of social welfare and industrial relations.

In answer to a question, Mr. Pedler said that the total retainable for dividend payments is negotiated with the host government, having regard to both the balance of payments situation and the requirements of the company for the payments for maintenance imports and operational costs in Europe.

Reference was also made to the importance of pure research in improving productivity, citing the example of palm oil plantations in the Congo having an important economic and social effect in raising the productivity of local labour working their own plots.

Doubt was cast upon the efficacy of the development of manpower planning. Existing educational programmes appear to carry little relevance to projected manpower needs in the future.

Finally, Mr. Pedler felt that one of the more attractive developments in the relation between the public and private sectors in industrialisation might well be the contracting of projects from the government to private companies, under special conditions and for limited periods.

The Changes in Trading Relations Between Europe and Africa[1]

DR. C. J. VAN DER VAEREN

Introduction

In the following analysis of the commercial relations between Europe and Africa and of the changes that have taken place recently, we shall pay particular attention to the relations between, on the one hand, the European Economic Community (EEC) and, on the other, the African and Malagasy States (EAMA) which have been associated with it since 1958, viz. Burundi, Cameroun, the Central African Republic, Congo-Brazzaville, Congo-Kinshasha, the Ivory Coast, Dahomey, Gabon, Upper Volta, Madagascar, Mali, Mauritania, Niger, Rwanda, Senegal, Somalia, Chad and Togo. Since the beginning of this association, two of the African states have enlarged their geographical area following the achievement of independence of the parts previously under British control.[2] However, the enlargement of these two economies has had comparatively little effect on trade as a whole between the Common Market countries and the EAMA.

In reality, the association as a whole extends beyond the borders of the EAMA countries. A certain number of overseas territories and states which are politically dependent on member states of the EEC have a status of association almost identical with that of the EAMA, although remaining separate from it. Two of them are in Africa—French Somaliland and the Comores Islands. The others

[1] Translated from the French original by P. S. Tregear.
[2] 1 July 1960 for Somaliland: 1 October 1961 for Cameroun.

are found in other parts of the world—South America and Central America[3] and the Pacific Ocean.[4]

In addition to the associated countries and overseas territories, one must remember the Departments of France overseas[5] which follow the practice of France in the liberalisation of trade with the other five member states of the EEC. One of these departments (Réunion) is part of the African Zone.

Finally, it is necessary to mention the special case of Algeria: the trade of this country was, until 1962, subject to the rules applicable to trade between the member states, since Algeria was *de jure* a Department of metropolitan France. On gaining its independence in July 1962, Algeria did not join the Association but it has continued to enjoy the benefits of the measures of free-trade which the Six agreed upon among themselves. This state of affairs has, however, begun to feel the effect of restrictions imposed by some EEC countries since the beginning of 1966. On its side, Algeria established in 1963 a tariff system which granted preferential treatment to member states of the EEC, and more particularly to France. For our purposes, it will be convenient to include Algeria among the African countries which have a special relationship with the EEC, even though this relationship must not be confused with that of EAMA.

To all intents and purposes, the legal regulations which control trade are the same for the independent EAMA states and for the countries and territories which maintain special political relationships with one or other of the member states of the EEC. Nevertheless, the group of the eighteen EAMA countries, that is to say practically speaking 'Associated Africa', represents by far the most important part of trade between EEC and the whole of the overseas associated countries.

[3] St. Pierre et Miquelon, and the Dutch West Indies which enjoy internal self-government and joined the Association on 1 October 1964 and 1 September 1962 respectively.

[4] New Caledonia, Wallis and Futuna Islands and French Polynesia. Dutch New Guinea, formerly an overseas territory in association, left the association on 1 October 1962 when its political status changed.

[5] French Guiana, Martinique, Guadeloupe and Réunion.

As regards statistics of trade, we shall consider as a whole the exchange between the EEC and the EAMA. In certain cases, in order to gain a more complete view of trade between the EEC and Africa, we shall add to EAMA the overseas territories and departments belonging to the African zone, as well as Algeria. For ease of reference we shall call this grouping 'Associated Africa', without this term being taken to refer exclusively to the Yaounde Convention.[6]

Indeed, this statistical grouping corresponds not only to a geographical situation but also to historical facts and judicial relations. The system of external trade between the EEC and these diverse groups of African countries is related to the same general principle which permeates the association. This principle is concerned with

1. the role which external trade can play in economic development and
2. the form which should be taken, in consequence, by commercial relations between wealthy, industrialised countries on the one hand and developing countries on the other.

In this paper we shall examine in turn the institutional and juridical framework of trade between the EEC and Associated Africa and then the actual development of exchange between these partners since the beginning of the association. These two aspects should help to foster discussion: this is not the place to draw *a priori* conclusions now.

I. The System of Commercial Exchange: The Association

In order to understand properly the system of trade relations between the EEC and associated Africa, we must go back to the general aims which were the basis of the establishment of the European Economic Community. In the field of trade, these aims were, on the one hand, to abolish the barriers which divide Europe so as to promote economic and social progress in the countries concerned and, on the other hand, to establish a common trade

[6] Nigeria is omitted in this study as its special association was agreed only on 16 July 1966.

policy towards other countries in order to make a better contribution to the progressive lessening of restrictions in international trade (see preamble to the Treaty of Rome).

The Association is founded on the same general principle of the factors of progress and of international trade relations, while bearing in mind at the same time both the wide gap between the level of economic and technological development in Europe and Africa and of the close relationship which already existed before 1958 between the associated countries and certain European countries.

In the present section we shall examine first the rules which govern trade within the association; then we shall see how these rules have worked since 1958; finally we shall show that the association does not aim at establishing a closed system and that the development of trade has broadened beyond the Six and the associated countries.

(a) THE LEGAL REGULATIONS GOVERNING TRADE

In the words of the Treaty of Rome, the association, agreed on by the six European contracting powers, has a double purpose:

1. 'the promotion of the economic and social development of the countries and territories' associated (i.e. 'to foster the interests of the inhabitants of these countries and territories and their prosperity in such manner as to lead them to the economic, social and cultural development that they expect');
2. 'the establishment of close economic relations between them and the Community as a whole' (Treaty of Rome, Article 131).[7]

[7] References to texts governing the association are as follows:
Treaty of Rome: TR.
Convention of application relating to the association of countries and territories overseas to the Community: CA.
Convention of Yaounde (renewing the association of the eighteen African and Malagasy states): CY.
The numbers which follow these abbreviations refer to articles.

If the respective nature and extent of these two objectives of the association are considered, the second appears, at least in large part, as a means directed towards the realisation of the first.

1. *The principles laid down by the Treaty of Rome*

The Treaty of Rome, which came into force on 1 January 1958, laid down some general principles for the liberalisation of trade with the aim of the progressive establishment of a great area of free-trade between all the member and associated states.

The Treaty stipulates that the six European countries must advance towards a customs 'disarmament' as regards products from the associated countries, by applying automatically to all of them the reductions in customs duty, as well as the relaxation of restrictive quotas, which they allow step by step to each other, so as to end in the complete abolition of barriers to imports after a transition period, fixed in principle at 12 years. (TR 133, para. 1.)

Normally the measures of liberalisation should come into operation progressively between Europe and Africa, as is the case among the six member states, in order to allow interested partners to adapt themselves to the currents of change which may develop.

The Treaty envisages, on the part of the associated countries, that there should be reciprocity in this progressive liberalisation. At the same time, the fiscal structure of these countries and their requirements for development may not permit them to practise a complete policy of free trade with the Six. In most of the associated countries liberalisation of trade must take above all the shape of equality of treatment applied to all members of the Community. (TR 133, paras. 2 and 4.) Bilateral preferential arrangements benefitting one of the Six must, accordingly, be extended to others, on the one hand, through a progressive reduction of discriminatory customs dues and, on the other hand, by the 'globalisation'[8] and

[8] 'In each country where there exist important quotas . . . the quotas open to States other than than that with which this country or territory has special relationship are transformed into global quotas available without discrimination to the other member States' (CA 11, para. 1).

progressive increase in the quotas open to the imports of member states other than that profiting from the privileged position. (CA 11).

It is true that the principle of the progressive elimination of tariff and quota barriers as between the associated countries and the whole of the EEC was laid down; but a characteristic of the association, in its trade aspect, is that the reciprocity of liberalising measures is asymmetrical. This is seen in the right granted only to the associated states to maintain or raise customs barriers against imports from the Community in order either to protect their own producers (e.g. in the case of new industries), or to collect additional public revenue, in the light of the importance of customs duties as a source of budgetary income in those countries. (TR 133, para. 3.) The condition for the exercise of this right is that there shall be no introduction of discrimination among the Six (TR 133, para. 5) nor, *a fortiori*, of any disadvantage for the Community in regard to third parties.

The Treaty of Rome also envisaged that the liberalisation of trade on the part of the associated countries should be directed, not only towards the six countries of the Common Market, but also towards all the co-associated states. One zone of free trade would, thus, at the end of the process of liberalisation, cover the whole area of the association.

2. *New factors contained in the Yaounde Convention*

The association is now regulated by the Yaounde Convention which was the result of negotiations conducted between the EEC and the eighteen African and Malagasy associated states (EAMA), now independent. The Convention came into force on 1 June 1964. It confirms, as a whole, the aims and principles laid down in the Treaty of Rome relating to the trade aspects of the association. Moreover, the association gave itself an important additional aim: the strengthening of the economic independence of the associated states.

In addition, the Convention emphasises that closer economic relations between the signatories should also aim at contributing to the development of international trade. (CY 1.)

The practical application of the liberalisation of trade is defined and emphasised in the Convention, in relation to the Treaty of Rome. First, it contains certain measures calculated to lift more completely and more rapidly the barriers to trade between the European and African partners.

On the European side, there has been accelerated liberalisation of trade with the associated countries in a number of raw tropical products: pineapples, coconuts, coffee, tea, pepper, vanilla, cloves, nutmegs and cocoa. (CY 2, para. 2.) These products at once enter duty-free into the Community if they originate in the associated countries; if they come from other countries, common customs duties are levied in the six member States.

For some agricultural products in the associated states, which compete with products in the member states, progress towards a common agricultural policy in EEC was likely to hinder exports from EAMA, in so far as this policy was one of protection for European producers. Therefore, the Yaounde Convention stipulated that the EEC should take particular consideration of the interests of the EAMA in such cases. (CY 11.) The privileged position of imports from the associated countries, therefore, now extends beyond the abolition of customs duties, of taxes of equivalent effect and restrictive quotas. We shall see below how this requirement of the Convention is brought into operation by the EEC.

On the African side the liberalisation of trade has been chiefly in two directions. The application of the rule of non-discrimination has been speeded up; it was due to become effective within 6 months of the signing of the convention (CY 3); it affects not only the customs duty on imports into EAMA but also the export dues (CY 4). As regards restrictive quotas on imports from the Six, the Yaounde Convention envisages their total disappearance within 4 years and not merely the progressive globalisation and increase in quota totals.

In general the Yaounde Convention affirms the principle of reciprocity between the Six and EAMA in the freeing of trade (CY 3, paras. 3 and 61) but this reciprocity is to remain asymmetrical. The African and Malagasy states reserve the right not to observe the liberalising rules on tariffs and quotas where necessary to meet their development and budget requirements. (CY 3, paras. 2, 3 and 6.) However, this right is not to be used in a way which would result in fresh discrimination either among the Six or to the disadvantage of the Community as a whole. Also, it is stipulated that the Six will enjoy most-favoured-nation treatment equally for imports and their products into the associated countries as for exports from these countries. (CY 4, para. 7.)

This last clause was all the more necessary since the EAMA countries are, as are all independent countries, in full control of their trade policy and are able, therefore, to extend to third parties (which could be competitors of the EEC) the measures of liberalisation taken in relation to EEC within the framework of the association.

The most-favoured-nation clause contains, however, an important loophole in favour of the development of intra-African trade. The EAMA have, in effect, the right to grant to other developing African countries a treatment more favourable even than that afforded to the Six either in the field of cross-frontier trade (CY 7) or by the conclusion of customs unions or of zones of free-trade. (CY 8 and 9.)

It would be thought that the desire to promote economic co-operation between developing countries would have led the contracting parties to envisage, in the Yaounde Convention as in the Treaty of Rome, the freeing of trade between the associated countries, parallel to that realised in the Six. The member states of the Community would, indeed, have been agreeable to such an arrangement: they so stated in their decision of 25 February 1964 renewing the association of dependent overseas countries and territories. On the contrary, the eighteen associated states have preferred not to regulate through the Yaounde Convention the trading arrangements which they would operate among themselves.

The Convention has thus put together a collection of measures which move towards the establishment of a whole series of zones of free trade between the EEC on the one hand and each of the associated States on the other. Nevertheless, there is in reality only one zone which has been formed with those African states which have established among themselves an effective customs union, as is the case with the Central African Customs and Economic Union, comprising the Camerouns, Congo-Brazzaville, Gabon, the Central African Republic and Chad.

(b) THE FREEING OF TRADE BETWEEN THE EEC AND THE EAMA

1. *Measures taken by the European countries*

Since the coming into force of the Treaty of Rome, the Six have applied to products coming from EAMA the same reductions in customs duties that they have granted among themselves. These measures have already reduced the level of duty levied, in successive stages from 1 January 1959 to 1 January 1966, by 60% for agricultural produce and by 80% for manufactured goods, in relation to the common customs tariff in the Six. By 1 January 1970 at the latest, the final date envisaged for the establishment of the Common Market, customs duties should be completely abolished. So, on the one hand, the associated countries will enjoy the same treatment for the entry of their products into the Community and, on the other hand, they will benefit, in relation to their competitors who are not associated, from the full margin of preference formed by the duties levied under the Common Customs Union. This advantage is greater for manufactured goods than for raw materials since, in the common customs tariff, duty will increase according to the degree of manufacture of the product. For raw materials the duty is most often nil.[9]

[9] Duty on the chief exports of EAMA to the Community is at present as follows:

12% for raw coffee,
6·7% for cocoa beans,
20% for bananas (Germany has an import quota with no duty),
10% for ground nut oil,
9% for palm oil and raw aluminium,
5% for tropical timbers,
0% for groundnuts, crude oil, raw rubber, cotton lint, oil cake, cobalt, diamonds, unrefined copper and gold.

Most of the duties are at present being reduced provisionally by one-fifth awaiting the result of the 'Kennedy Round' at GATT.

It is probable that the common external tariff will be subject to certain definitive reductions following their multilateral negotiations.

As regards quantitative restrictions, the global quotas allowed by the Six for products from the EAMA have already doubled in volume since 1958. They, too, are due to be entirely abolished by 1 January 1970 between the member states and between them and the overseas associated countries.

Agricultural produce is to form the subject of a special organisation of the market within the Community. How will the Six take into account the interests of the associated countries when they are exporting competitive products?

The Community has already operated a system for rice and processed products of cereals, rice and cassava. A provisional levy has been established for the import of these products into the Community. Its amount is reduced for rice imported from the associated countries for both polished and hulled rice. It is abolished, within the limits of certain quantities for processed products of cereals, rice or cassava from the associated countries.

As regards vegetable oils, of which several African countries are important exporters, the Community has recently reached a decision. Since oil seed from the associated countries will not be protected under the Common Tariff (no duty charged), it is proposed that where necessary special steps would be taken to ensure the continuity of their entry into the EEC.

2. *Measures taken by African countries*

Before the coming into force of the Yaounde Convention, the states of the Equatorial Customs Union (the former French Equatorial Africa) and Madagascar had already exempted the whole of the EEC from the application of their customs tariff which, however, remained applicable to third parties. The taxes of entry, on the contrary, remained of general application.

Under the Convention all the other associated overseas countries which operated a discriminatory system exempted the produce of the EEC from customs duty from 1 December 1964. Equality of treatment has thus been reached between the Six by applying uniformly the customs system previously enjoyed by the most favoured of the member states of the Community. In the overseas countries which form part of the franc zone, however, certain quantitative restrictions still place limits on imports from member states other than France. In addition, the attachment of many associated states to a monetary zone in common with France renders easier imports from France rather than from the other member states. The existence of long-established commercial and economic relations between some associated states and one or other European country, reduces still further the practical effect of non-discrimination in customs duty.

The application of non-discrimination between the Six involves only a partial liberalisation of trade between the EEC and the associated states for it affects only customs duties themselves, which have never been a major influence on imports from the former metropolitan power. Concerning liberalisation as regards the whole of the EEC, the Yaounde Convention requires a progressive reduction of 15% a year in the other dues and taxes having an effect equal to that of customs duties and levied on the entry of goods into the associated countries. Moreover, the quantitative restrictions, already globalised, are progressively reduced and should be abolished within 4 years after the coming into force of the Convention, i.e. in 1968. These two measures represent, for the associated countries, their response to customs disarmament undertaken in their regard by the member states of the EEC.

However, certain African states are exempted temporarily from the obligation to liberalise in this way their trade with the Six. These are Burundi, Congo-Kinshasha, Somalia and Togo, in which countries the former metropolitan powers had followed the same trade policy *erga omnes* by virtue of their international undertaking which required free competition in the mandated territories and in the Congo Basin. This situation is only provisional for it is generally agreed that the treaties in question were binding on the contracting powers but that they did not so bind the African states which have since gained independence. Thus, Cameroun and the countries of the former French Equatorial Africa have brought into operation a common customs agreement comprising, alongside common taxes of entry, customs duties which are not applied to EEC. Rwanda has recently established a customs tariff of the same type (known as 'the two-column tariff'). The position of the four other African associated countries who do not yet offer preferential treatment to the Six is to be re-examined at the latest in 1967; that is to say that it has been regarded as provisional since the signing of the Yaounde Convention (cf. Article 61).

The principle of reciprocity in the liberalisation of trade between the European and African partners in the association is diluted, as we have seen above, by an important reservation in favour of the associated countries only. Several associated countries have already exercised their right to set up new customs barriers, even in relation to the Six, chiefly with the aim of facilitating their own industrialisation. Thus, the Ivory Coast has restricted the import of refined petroleum products since her refinery came into production at Abidjan. In order to protect its assembly plants, Senegal has placed restrictions on the entry of certain motor vehicles. This country has also, quite recently, increased the duty on cotton textiles and on iron and steel sheet. The Malagasy Republic has taken the same action over various articles produced by its national industries. In addition, several associated states have increased *erga omnes* the entry dues on certain luxury products, such as spirits, for revenue purposes.

(c) THE EXTENSION OF LIBERALISATION OUTSIDE THE ASSOCIATION

The association is far from being a closed system. Indeed, the measures of non-discrimination and liberalisation lead to the formation of multilateral preferential relations, especially where there previously existed bilateral agreements; this is already a clear broadening of the exchange system. The contracting parties have, moreover, taken care not to construct, in principle, a watertight zone of preferential trade between the Six and Associated Africa. The extension of trade outside the association proceeds within EEC as well as within EAMA.

1. *European aspects of extension*

The Treaty of Rome already authorised certain member states to maintain important sources of supply for tropical products outside the African associated countries, without applying the common customs tariff. Thus, duty-free quotas have been granted for the importing of bananas into Germany and of coffee beans into Benelux and Italy. In the Yaounde Convention, duty-bearing quotas have been abolished on coffee but the Benelux countries have been authorised to charge temporarily an entry duty low in comparison with that of the common customs tariff. (CY 2, para. 3.) These special measures concern particularly the exporting countries of South and Central America.

Following the conclusion of the Yaounde Convention, the member States of EEC have, in addition, decided to extend to all the tropical countries a reduction in import duties on the following products: tropical timbers, tea, pineapples, coconuts, coffee, pepper, vanilla, cloves, cocoa and nutmegs. Since 1 January 1964 the first two of these products have been admitted duty free irrespective of source of origin.

In general, moreover, the customs policy of EEC aims at promoting wider exchange with third party countries. It must not be forgotten that the common customs tariff gives a level of protection far lower than that of the customs system of the EEC's principal industrial competitors, namely the U.K. and the U.S.A.[10] The margin of preference enjoyed by imports from the associated countries into EEC is therefore not very great. We shall see later that it is

[10] This is clearly seen from the following comparative statistics:

	Average duties on imports	Structure of customs tariff: proportion of duties of	
		more than 25%	more than 35%
EEC	11·7%	5%	0·05%
U.S.A.	17·8%	28%	10 %
U.K.	18·4%	31%	2 %

The Common Customs Tariff referred to here is that of 1962, excluding the provisional reduction of one-fifth.

insufficient, by itself, to effect significant changes in the current of trade to the benefit of the associated countries.

Finally, it should be noted that the preferential system of the Yaounde Convention is not a closed shop: the association is open. The Convention itself envisages that other states 'whose economic structure and production are comparable to those of the associated States' will be able to adhere to the agreement of association. (CY 58.) Moreover, the member states of EEC have solemnly declared themselves to be ready to conclude special agreements of association or simple trade agreements with the other developing countries, if they so request.[11] It goes without saying, of course, that the African states who were signatories of the Yaounde Convention must be consulted over any new request for association.

In this way, EEC has already established a free-trade area with Nigeria. Within the agreement reached with this country can be found the application of the principle of reciprocal but asymmetrical liberalisation between EEC and the less-developed partner. Negotiations have also been started with the three English-speaking East African countries, and with Morocco and Tunisia.

2. *African aspects of extension*

Just as the Six may, as described above, extend to countries other than their overseas associates the customs preferences enjoyed by the latter, the Yaounde Convention does not require the associated countries to levy protective duties or restrictive quotas on third party countries. We have seen that the few associated countries who operate a single, non-discriminatory customs tariff may, at least temporarily, refrain from granting preference to the EEC. It is clearly very doubtful that the principle of reciprocity in the liberalisation of trade would be observed if this situation became definitive, or if other associated countries abandoned *erga omnes* and for all products the application of their customs tariff.

Nevertheless, the associated countries are free to grant to certain third-party states the customs system enjoyed by the Six through the conclusion of customs unions or of zones of free-trade. These

[11] Declaration of intention of 1 and 2 April 1963.

agreements, however, must not be incompatible with the principles of the Convention. Incompatibility would be present, for example, if such agreements permitted evasion of the common customs tariff through the bad faith of one of the associated states. Two concrete cases already exist where this problem could be raised: Mali has suspended the application of its customs duties on products coming from Eastern European countries; Congo-Brazzaville has granted duty-free imports to the Soviet Union. There is, however, no *a priori* objection to such agreements.

2. Trade within the Framework of the Association in Relation to World Trade

The fundamental problems of the associated countries are very similar to those of most countries which are little or non-industrialised and, in particular, with those of the other relatively undeveloped African countries. They have an urgent need to increase their productivity and the real income they derive from it. For this they must, among other things, increase their imports in order to equip themselves and, at the same time, develop their income from exports in order to ensure payment, immediate or deferred, for these imports. In this field they have to face the acute problem of the long-term worsening of the terms of trade for primary products. This phenomenon, moreover, concerns not only tropical producers but also, within the industrialised economies, the primary sector in relation to the secondary and tertiary sectors.

In the field of trading relations, the associated countries have a second fundamental need, that of a relative stability in their revenue to meet the wide short-term fluctuations in price which are suffered by raw materials on the world markets. Usually these changes in price are out of proportion to the variation in quantities produced in relation to demand.

(a) THE PRINCIPLES OF ORGANISATION OF INTERNATIONAL TRADE

Before the formation of the association, the principles of international trade most widely accepted were those contained in the

General Agreement on Trade and Tariffs (GATT), signed in 1947 by many industrialised countries. The rules of good trading conduct thus established on the international plane are to be found essentially in the 'most-favoured-nation' clause which aimed at a multilateral and reciprocal freeing of trade. The only limitation to this basic principle, contained in Article XXIV, was the right of establishing zones of free-trade. One of the parties to the agreement was, by this, entitled not to extend to all its fellow-contractors the measures of liberalisation when these consisted of a total and reciprocal abolition of trade barriers with one or several other countries. Nevertheless, there was a safeguard, namely that the free-trade areas established should not 'constitute obstacles to the trade of the other contracting parties with the partners in the area'. The agreement here contains an ambiguity if not a contradiction, for either this safeguard must not be taken literally or else it annulled the right to establish zones of free-trade, except in marginal cases where the partner member of GATT is the sole importer or exporter of a single product.

Moreover, in 1947, world economic conditions were very different from those obtaining after the period of post-war reconstruction. Thus it was not surprising that, at that time, the special problems of the developing countries were not taken into account as such and that the system of world trade was established in the fashion most favourable to industrialised economies. Many relatively less-developed countries, which have since become independent one after the other, were not taken in by this and have refused to sign the 1947 agreement despite the blandishments of the contracting powers.

However, in 1963, and under pressure from the United States, GATT examined more closely the problem of commercial relations between the developing and the industrialised countries. All the partners, both the industrialised and those developing, who had signed the agreement, were of one mind in declaring that the elimination of all customs barriers could bring about a rapid solution to the problems of development in the least favoured countries. The doctrine of complete liberalisation in international trading relations was thus reaffirmed as being of general validity.

However, in recent years various fundamental criticisms have been widely raised against this doctrine, from the point of view of defence of the interests of less-developed countries.

The first of these criticisms holds that the principle of full reciprocity in the freedom of trade between partners who are unequal in economic strength intensifies, or at least maintains, the economic dependence of the less-developed countries concerned. This had already been clearly seen by the German economist Friedrich List, who wrote in 1827: 'To persist in trading freely with societies or organisations more advanced than oneself, is to fall under their guardianship, to remain in a state of stagnation.'

More liberal world trade may well encourage an increase in the sales of raw materials by relatively less-developed countries, but this would reinforce at the same time their dependence on the export of one or a few products and, in consequence, render their economies more vulnerable to the ravages of world markets.

The second criticism of the doctrine of general free-trade is that, if all customs barriers are reduced equally, regardless of the level of economic development, the keener competition between the exporting countries would, because of the structure of the so-called world markets, not be of so great a benefit to them as to the giant trading nations who control these markets.

The third criticism, which is perhaps the most important, is that a general and undifferentiated liberalisation of trade would lead to an increase in competition between the industrialised countries to export their finished and half-finished goods and that it would, in consequence, reduce the opportunity for industrialisation in the less-developed countries by limiting the markets in which they would be able to sell their new products.

Again, the principle of universal free-trade is open to grave doubt if it is remembered that most industrialised countries, some of whom claim to be the most forthright advocates of the liberty of exchange, do not apply this principle within their own national economy, since this would entail—and so did, especially in the nineteenth century—unbearable social consequences, at least among the weaker sectors of the economy. This situation may be the result of various factors, either that the sector concerned is split into many small units in the face of monopolies or cartels, or that its technical progress has lagged behind that of others. It is well known that, in industrialised economies, relative incomes are not the result of the workings of simple competition between the economic agents. Competition is regulated by public power.

These criticisms of the doctrine of universal free-trade raised by the less-developed countries contain as a constructive element certain new principles for economic relations between the industrialised powers and the developing countries. These principles may be summed up as, on the one hand, the establishment of stable and organised markets for at least those raw materials of greatest concern to the developing countries and, on the other, the setting-up of unilateral—or, according to circumstances, asymmetrical—trade barriers to the benefit of developing countries. Recently a further solution has been suggested in place of the first of these principles. It is the establishment of a system of financial compensation designed to maintain the export revenue of less developed economies at the level normally desired. This solution is, however, without long-term validity since only a relatively short-lived disequilibrium can be adjusted in this manner without the system ending in quasi-permanent subsidies for certain exports. Moreover, if such a system operated in one case it would lead to an emphasis in imbalance in various sectors between supply and demand for primary products. It would thus increase, on a world scale, the kind of difficulties which at present confront certain countries in the franc zone because of the dismantling, over several years, of the system of quotas of delivery and of *sur-prix*. These countries have to make a much greater effort to adjust themselves to the general conditions of world markets than if they had been forced by the laws of the market to a continuous adaptation.

(b) THE RESOLUTIONS OF UNCTAD AND THE DEVELOPMENT OF GATT

The principles of the organisation of trade between the industrialised and the less-developed countries which have been worked out to amend the doctrine of universal free-trade have recently taken concrete form, at least in a general aspect, in Chapter 4 which was added to the General Agreement (GATT) in 1965, as well as in the resolutions of the Conference of the United Nations for Trade and Commerce (UNCTAD). At the present stage, this new system of trade is little more than a declaration of intent: its rules of application are vaguely sketched on a world scale.

The new Article XXXVI of GATT contains, in essence, three principles. First, it envisages the right of less-developed countries to take special measures, that is to raise new customs barriers of a specific nature with the aim of stimulating their trade and development. Secondly, when relatively developed countries negotiate over the raising or lowering of trade barriers in the framework of bilateral or multilateral liberalisation of trade, the less-developed countries concerned are not required to grant to them reciprocal measures of relaxation in a way which would harm their development, finances or trade. This second principle can be summed up as 'asymmetrical reciprocity'. The third principle states the necessity of stabilising and improving on world markets the position of raw materials, at least of those which concern particularly the developing countries.

The new Chapter 4 of GATT has been signed by five of the six member states of EEC, France having abstained. The reason for this abstention is not that France disagrees with the three principles contained in Chapter 4; on the contrary, France wished to go further along the line followed by the conference, particularly in practical application. In fact, the rules of application of Article XXXVI which are deemed to be contained in the new Article XXXVIII of the General Agreement are too vague to be effective. The additional French proposals may be summed up as: on the one hand, the necessity that developed economies should grant certain preferences in trade to less-developed countries, with the aim of promoting the latter's exports; and, on the other hand, the need to organise not only trade but also the production of primary products.

(c) THE PLACE AND FUTURE OF THE ASSOCIATION

The association established at the Yaounde Convention is an attempt to put into operation, on a regional basis, principles of trade relations similar to those drawn up recently on a world scale by UNCTAD and GATT. It contains in effect a series of measures designed to liberalise exchange and combining, on one hand, the improvement of marketing machinery and, on the other, inequality in reciprocal concessions in favour of the less-developed partners with the aim of aiding the latter to develop and, in particular, to industrialise.

The working of the association does not form an obstacle to the progressive organisation of a system which would permit at one and the same time a general expansion of world trade and the development of the less-favoured nations. Indeed, the partners in the association, European as well as African and Malagasy, have many times declared that the system was merely transitional and that it could be extended in due course to the whole of trade relations in the free world or be replaced by a different international system which would guarantee at least equal advantage to the partners. It is symptomatic in this respect that UNCTAD should have adopted in 1964 a recommendation proposed by the developing nations according to which existing special preferences should come to an end in 1970 *on condition that* the less-developed countries had in the meantime obtained at least equivalent advantages within the framework of a world trade organisation.

The transitional nature of the association's system is reflected, in a practical manner, in the fact that agreements of association, equally with the Eighteen as with Nigeria, are concluded only for a maximum period of 5 years and that they are due to expire in every case in mid-1969.

The system of association envisages a series of special measures designed to help certain associated countries to put themselves in a state of readiness to participate, at the end of the period of association, in a satisfactory world-trade organisation and thus to enjoy wider and diversified trading relations. Before the period of association, on the contrary, these countries had developed a good part of their production and trade in a hot-house atmosphere within the franc zone. They would, therefore, have been incapable of meeting, without a period of transition, international competition which would most certainly have been a brake on their development.[12]

To this end, the Yaounde Convention has made provision, in favour of the associated countries, for special aid towards 'production and diversification'. The aim is, first of all, to develop in the associated countries those products for which there are potential outlets. Secondly, it is a matter of rendering existing products more competitive by increasing yield and improving marketing conditions so that cost price is reduced to a level compatible with the balance between supply and demand on world markets. The third aim is towards a better internal balance of the countries which had previously been orientated particularly towards the economy of the metropolitan power.

The progressive establishment of the free circulation of goods within the EEC prevents the maintenance of two different systems of purchase with the associated countries: purchase by France of a series of tropical products[13] at fixed prices and in fixed quantities and purchase by the other member states according to their needs of the moment and to supplies available. The system of association is based on the choice of the system of competition. This posed, for many associated African states, a very large problem of adaptation to the conditions of world markets. In so far as they previously enjoyed *sur-prix* in their protected market, they had to make a special effort to reduce their export selling price, and consequently their cost price.

The line taken on world prices was decided after the negotiations of the Yaounde Convention. In order to allow the countries concerned to adapt their system of production and marketing, a special arrangement of aid was set up for the 5 year period covered by the Convention. This aid served to finance the structural improve-

[12] Section 3, (a) p. 105.

[13] Coffee, Groundnuts, groundnut oil, palm oil, coconut, cotton, pepper, rice, sugar, gum-arabic. Bananas have therefore not been taken into consideration in spite of their previously protected markets in France and in Italy.

ment of the exporting sectors so as to render them competitive. Since such an improvement can only bear fruit progressively over several years, it is supplemented by decreasing subsidies designed to fill the gap between the cost and that price eventually realised within each exporting economy. It is to be hoped that in this way the export revenue of the associated countries will not be reduced as a consequence of adaptation to the conditions of world competition.

It should be added that these aids to existing export production are supplemented again by credits, in the form of grants or loans, designed specifically to finance the initiation or development of new products so as to diversify the economies of the associated countries and to make them, in this way, less vulnerable to the fluctuations in revenue gained from a small range of principal exports.

The fixing of attention on the world market brings with it a particular danger for the associated countries when the conditions of competition on that market do not reflect accurately the real situation of supply and demand for the products concerned. Thus, the market in vegetable oils is influenced in marked manner by the effect of by-products whose production is a function of other demands. The share of these by-products in the total supply of vegetable oils is tending to increase steeply: it has risen from 20% in 1950 to 38% in 1962. For the associated African countries the chief competitor in this field is soya oil, resulting from the production of cattle cake which itself is a function of the demand for meat, particularly in industrialised countries.

In this way the organisation of the market for vegetable oils in the Community provides for a new type of aid for seeds and oils produced in the associated countries. When world prices fall below a level fixed annually, EEC will grant to the exporting associated countries subsidies which fill the gap between the agreed level and the world market price. These subsidies will, moreover, be on a decreasing scale so that they do not absolve the producing countries from making lasting changes in the relation between supply and demand.

Wider access to the world market brings with it, for the associated countries, another risk, that of sudden fluctuations in price. These are the result of speculation which is very much a function of the inelasticity of short-term supply (when it is not a matter of the value of the currencies in which transactions are made). The Yaounde Convention also provides for a special type of aid to meet the evil effects such fluctuations bring to bear on the financial equilibrium of the associated countries; the European Development Fund is now empowered to make advances to their stabilisation funds.

The object of the various measures of financial and technical co-operation in trade matters is therefore to make possible, in the future, either the extension to other parts of the world of an organised system of liberalisation of trade, or to integrate both the member states and the associated countries in an international trade organisation which would have results at least as satisfactory as the system of association.

In its successive developments, the EEC never loses sight of the fact that one of the fundamental aims of its establishment is the development of world trade. Thus, the formation of an association with certain countries towards whom the member states had special historical responsibilities does not prevent it from taking account, as far as is humanly possible, of the interests of the less-developed countries who are not part of that association.

The EEC co-operates actively in the organisation of international markets for the chief basic products. The Yaounde Convention itself provides that the member and associated states shall consult each other 'with a view to undertaking in common agreement appropriate action on an international scale to resolve the problems posed by the flow and marketing of tropical products'. (Protocol No. 4, para. 3.)

As a concrete example one may quote the recent proposals of the Commission of the EEC towards an international agreement on cereals. These proposals contain four major points: the search for international balance in the supply and demand for cereals; the establishment of stable prices at a level satisfactory to producers; suitable access to markets for all producers with a view to the extension of world trade; and, lastly, the possibility of granting special consideration to the interests of the less-developed participants.

Together with this position taken in respect of international markets, the EEC has, unilaterally, taken steps in the interest of less-developed exporting countries which are not included in the association. Thus in 1965, 40% of the products imported by the Community from developing countries were exempt from entry charges. In addition, in cases where the exports of less-developed countries were nevertheless likely to be handicapped by its trade policy, the Community negotiates special trade agreements to meet these difficulties. Such agreements have already been made with the following third-party states: Iran, Israel and Lebanon. These agreements carry tariff reductions; that with Lebanon also includes the most-favoured-nation clause.

This overture to third-party developing nations can take an even more concrete form, as we have seen above, through the conclusion of special agreements of association such as that signed on 16 July 1966 between the EEC and Nigeria.

3. Recent Structural Changes in Trade between EEC and Africa

Having described the economy and operation of the system of exchange within the European–African association, we should now attempt to describe within the present situation the influence of the association on trade, first between the EEC and the EAMA and, then, between these two groups and their other principal partners.

In reality, although the data reveal certain fairly clear tendencies, one can only draw from them provisional conclusions. They cover only the 8 years of association (1958-65); over such a short period a combination of factors may conceal fundamental tendencies. In particular, the statistics covering the whole of the EAMA are clearly affected by the slump in economic activity in Congo-Kinshasha after independence in mid-1960. The same is true for the contraction in Algerian trade after its independence in 1962.

Furthermore, the position of the African associated countries has changed markedly during the period under consideration. Between 1960 and 1962 the majority of them achieved independence and have thus become in control of their own trade policy. They have profited from this position by reaching bilateral trade agreements outside the association.

Finally, if the basic principles regulating trade between the EEC and the associated countries have remained the same since the Treaty of Rome, their application has modified the conditions which determine trade. The bringing into operation of the juridical framework and of concrete measures is far from being completed. The tariff and quota situation has been changed only in small steps since 1958. Measures of aid to production are still in the second or third of their five annual stages. As for the common agricultural policy, which concerns the associated nations under more than one head, the detailed regulations still cover only certain groups of products.

We shall recall what was the state of affairs before the formation of the association. Then, we shall examine the changes that have taken place in the external trade of the EEC with Africa and the rest of the world, and of trade between EAMA and the Six and others. In this last section we shall look in closer detail at the development of some of the principal exports of the associated African states in order to understand better the effect of the association on their trade.

(a) THE DIRECTION OF TRADE BETWEEN EEC AND AFRICA BEFORE THE ASSOCIATION

Before the setting up of an association between EEC and the overseas countries and territories maintaining 'special relationships' with some of the Six, trade between the countries of the future 'Common Market' was clearly determined by the existence of these 'relationships'. The result was a wide variety in the economic situation and trade structure of the future associates.

In 1956-7, 65% of the trade of the territories of 'Associated Africa' was with their respective metropolitan powers. For those tied to their metropolitan centres by a preferential system the share rose to 72% for both imports and exports. On the other hand, in those countries which practised the open-door policy, trade with the metropolis dropped to 54% for exports and to only 40% for imports.

In the geographical orientation of trade, EEC countries other than the metropolis occupied a significant place only in those African associated countries which were not part of a preferential system; the share in these cases was of the order of 16% for imports and 18% for exports. Excluding trade with the metropolis, the countries bound to the latter through preferences did little trade with the future partners in the Common Market; at a level of 5% and 6% for imports and exports respectively.

These preferential systems of exchange which had been in existence for 50 years did not consist only of customs tariff preference. France granted also to the African countries which were tied politically to her a guaranteed market, in quantity and in price, for their exports of raw materials. Italy did the same for bananas from Somaliland. The main exportable products of these countries were thus directed, not towards world markets but towards those of a monetary zone and, in particular, to that of the governing European power who fixed import quotas in accordance with the needs of its consumers and of its industry. Prices in these bilateral markets were sheltered from the fluctuations of supply and demand, at least in the short term, in other countries. They could be fixed in regard to the need to ensure a satisfactory return to the rural African producer.

For most of the raw materials in countries tied to France, only the quantity produced for export in excess of the fixed quota had eventually to find an outlet on world markets, at a price determined by the conditions of the moment. In such cases the world market represented only a marginal outlet. Prices on the world market had become progressively lower, taking good years with bad, than the contract prices with France. In 1960 the margin of the supplement paid by France was, for example, 30-50% for coffee, 50-70% for bananas, 10-35% for groundnuts, 150-300% for pepper.[14]

In return, the African countries in the franc zone paid higher prices than those in free-trade areas for a good number of food products and manufactured goods imported from their metropolis

[14] Reference: *Marchés tropicaux*, 16 January 1960.

or other countries in the same zone. Products from outside the franc zone were subject to discriminatory tax on entry, which reduced competition. A study made in 1961 revealed a margin of 'supplementation' of 58% for food imports as a whole (rising to 80% for wheat and sugar) and of 17% for raw textiles and 35% for cotton print.

The system of commercial exchange established in the association has clearly had to take careful account of the main channels already existing between the Six of the Market and the African countries concerned, and particularly of the market system organised and protected within the franc zone, to which belonged the great majority of the countries of 'associated Africa'. These structures could not be demolished without causing great damage to the African economies involved.

The establishment of an association between the latter and the Six must be able, rather, to ensure a progressive evolution which would be compatible with the existence of the new European Economic Community and meet the requirements of the associated countries for their development. It must be remembered, indeed, that these countries are among those of the undeveloped world which have come the latest to economic adolescence and where the infra-structure for development is, on the whole, the weakest.

(b) THE DEVELOPMENT OF TRADE BETWEEN EEC AND AFRICA

From 1958 to 1965 the external trade of the EEC countries, imports and exports, has risen in value by 112%, while world trade (excluding the Soviet bloc) rose by 72%. The EEC would thus appear to be a particularly dynamic element in world trade; trade within the Community itself alone has tripled in value in the course of these 8 years! In volume, the increases are evidently a little less: world trade increased by 69%; that of the EEC with the rest of the world by 74%, and intra-EEC exchange by 192%. During the same period the geographical distribution of trade has developed as shown in Table 1.

TABLE 1. Development of the Trade of EEC: 1958-65
(in 000,000 *unités de compte*)

	Imports		Exports		Increase/ Decrease	
	1958	1965	1958	1965	Imports	Exports
World (excl. EEC)	16,098	28,566	15,872	27,083	+ 77%	+71%
Total DC (a)	6813	10,523	6195	7506	+ 55%	+22%
of which OA (b)	1600	2046	1918	1733	+ 28%	—10%
Associated Africa (c)	913	1146	713	827	+ 26%	+16%
Non-assoc. Africa (d)	1049	2195	951	1528	+109%	+61%

(a) Developing countries including Africa (except the South African Republic).
(b) "Overseas Associates", i.e. states, territories and countries in the association, overseas Departments of France, plus Algeria.
(c) The associated African states and Madagascar.
(d) Excluding South Africa and Algeria (special trade agreement with EEC).
Reference: EEC, *Monthly Statistics of External Trade,* 1966, No. 8-9.

1. Trade with the developing nations as a whole has increased a little less swiftly than with the industrialised nations; this is particularly noticeable in the case of exports from the EEC to them, which have risen by only 22%. In actual fact these exports had already increased appreciably in 1960 and 1961, but in 1962 they fell back to the 1958 level.

2. Among the developing countries, those with special trading relations with the EEC[15] have increased less than the others their share as suppliers to the Six; as clients of the Community their share even fell from 1958 to 1965 while that of the other developing nations increased. Nevertheless, it must be noted that Algeria, which in 1958 took 54% of the EEC exports to the overseas associates, received only 33% of that total in 1965. If the Algerian case is excluded, EEC exports to the recognised overseas associates have risen during the period under consideration by 38%, or more than those to the rest of the undeveloped world.

[15] For simplification, we are labelling this collection of states, centres, territories, and departments 'Overseas Associates', although some of them are not legally associated (cf. Introduction).

3. The contrast in the development of trade with the associated countries and with the non-associated countries is particularly striking if one looks at Africa by itself. The EEC has considerably increased its imports from North Africa and non-associated tropical Africa; the rate of increase is noticeably greater than that of purchases of the EEC from other countries and it is more than three times that of imports of products from associated Africa. As for exports from the EEC to Africa, it should be noticed that these have increased much less swiftly than imports. Again we find the same difference between the associated and the non-associated countries: trade relations between the EEC and non-associated Africa have intensified much faster than with associated Africa. For Africa as a whole the Six increased their purchases almost twice as fast as their sales.

Finally, if we examine how EEC imports have developed by groups of products, it appears that the most marked increase is to be found in petroleum products (see Table 2). In 1958 the EEC bought from Africa only 1% of its supplies of energy; this share has risen to 20% in 1965 thanks chiefly to the source of supply which has been created in Algeria and Libya.

TABLE 2. Indices of Imports in EEC by Groups of Products in 1965
1958=100

Source	World (a)	Developing countries (b)	Africa		
			assoc. (EAMA)	non-assoc. (c)	Algeria
Food, drink and tobacco	155	125	104	112	50
Energy	163	186	200	2200	4650
Raw materials	142	137	125	140	87
Chemical and manufactured goods	232	221	172	212	80

(a) Trade outside EEC.
(b) Including Africa but not South Africa.
(c) Excluding South Africa and Algeria.
N.B.: the indices are calculated by value.

For each of the other broad categories of products, the non-associated countries of Africa have improved their position as providers to the EEC more than the associated countries. The difference between the two groups of African countries is most noticeable in industrial products. However, since the demand of the EEC for these products is the one which is increasing most rapidly and since aid to the development of the associated countries is now applied particularly to their industrialisation, these countries will probably be able to increase more swiftly in the future their sales to the EEC of manufactured or processed products.

(c) THE DEVELOPMENT OF THE TRADE OF 'ASSOCIATED AFRICA' WITH THE SIX AND WITH THE REST OF THE WORLD

It is more difficult to assess the development of the external trade of the associated countries than that of the EEC because the statistics for 1965 are as yet incomplete for certain African countries.[16] The total external trade of EAMA has increased, between 1958 and 1965, by one quarter, both as regards imports and exports. As far as trade relations between the EEC and EAMA are concerned a reverse tendency can be seen, from the African point of view, from that noted in the examination of the development of European trade: the EEC has kept its relative position as supplier to the EAMA (65% in 1958, 63% in 1965) while it has regressed as purchaser (72% in 1958, but only 59% in 1965).

Taken as a whole, the EEC remains by far the chief purchaser of the products of the EAMA. Its market absorbs growing amounts of produce from the associated African states; in 1964 the increase was of the order of 50%, by volume, compared with 1958. However, just as the Six have increased their sales to other countries to a greater extent than they have to the African associated countries, the latter have developed more rapidly their outlets beyond the EEC than they have within it. It is obviously easier to increase the importance of relatively restricted channels of trade than to enlarge

[16] We have therefore to use those given for 1964 for the following countries: Congo-Kinshasha (Imports), Upper Volta and Somalia.

yet further one's share in a market in which one already holds a dominant position.

Sales of the EAMA outside the EEC have grown particularly in the field of phosphates, coffee, groundnuts, oil and cotton. On the other hand, the EEC has become a more important outlet for cobalt, palm oil and cocoa (see Table 3). It should again be noted that,

TABLE 3. Principal Exports from the EAMA to the World and to the EEC: Developments from 1958 to 1964 (a)
000 tons

	1958		1964		World changes	EEC share	
	World	EEC	World	EEC	64/58	1958	1964
Mineral ore	—	—	4983	3368	—	—	68%
Phosphates	62	62	1523	744	+1456%	100%	49%
Maganese ore	321	140	1231	?	+284%	44%	?
Crude petroleum	450	450	1147	1035	+155%	100%	90%
Aluminium	22	?	49	46	+121%	?	94%
Timber	1473	1228	3070	2535	+108%	83%	83%
Cocoa	116	79	217	175	+88%	68%	80%
Bananas	204	198	368	347	+80%	97%	94%
Diamonds	3·9	3	5·4	0·8	+40%	2%	15%
Coffee	268	210	369	184	+38%	78%	50%
Rubber	40	23	47	23	+17%	58%	50%
Cotton	85	83	98	63	+15%	98%	64%
Groundnut oil	121	111	135	129	+12%	92%	95%
Cattle cake	251	185	233	162	—7%	74%	69%
Groundnuts	469	441	382	315	—19%	94%	83%
Palm oil	183	147	146	143	—20%	80%	98%
Palm kernels	151	146	111	109	—27%	97%	98%
Cobalt	9·8	5·9	7·1	7·1	—28%	61%	100%
Gold	17·1	17·1	9·2	9·2	—46%	100%	100%
Copper	242	216	75	75	—69%	89%	100%

(a) The statistics for 1965 are not yet sufficiently complete for use.
Reference: EEC, *Statistics of External Trade of the Associated Countries.*

among the exports of the African associated states, mineral products have generally grown at a clearly faster rate than agricultural products. In fact, the production of several items began only in the fifties—iron ore, phosphates, oil and aluminium. Congo-Kinshasha is the principal exporter of certain minerals: the rate of increase for diamonds is low, that for cobalt, copper and gold is negative. The conditions of supply in the EAMA countries in this way determine the variation in exports, at least as much as, if not more than, the availability of outlets.

As for agricultural exports, these have grown especially in those products for which demand increases fastest in the wealthier countries, i.e. timber, cocoa, bananas and coffee. Nevertheless, here also one must take account of the changes which have taken place in production, particularly to explain the decrease in exports of oil cake, palm oil and palm kernels.

The EAMA countries have up to now gained particular advantage over the Common Market for those products of which their total exports have increased the most (timber, cocoa, oil, phosphates and bananas). For only one of the products under consideration—cocoa—has the Common Market become a more important purchaser than others at the same time as the EAMA improved its position as supplier to the Six. On the other hand, where total exports have decreased, the decrease generally affects less sales to the EEC than to other countries; thus the Common Market appears to be a more stable outlet (cf. the case for palm oil, palm kernels, cobalt and copper).

The statistics given above do not reveal any decisive influence coming from preferential customs tariffs. The degree of preference written into the system of association will help the countries associated to increase their exports while taking other indispensable steps, such as increasing the quantity of production, improving its processing, the regularity of supply, the efficiency of marketing procedure as well as of sales promotion in the markets of the importing countries.

The working of these measures and the reduction in the level of cost prices through rationalisation in the associated countries are helped by the Community through financial and technical co-operation. Their results must be felt, in the long run, in the trading position of the associated countries on the world market. Furthermore, if these countries are to draw the maximum benefit for their development, this market must be organized in such a way as to ensure more satisfactory and stable incomes to the exporting countries of the developing part of the world.

Conclusion

The contractual association of the eighteen African and Malagasy states with the European Economic Community is a product of historical circumstances. Without taking them into account it is impossible to understand and judge the principles which govern trade within the association; nor can one interpret the statistics of the development of trade between Europe and Africa. During the colonial epoch, the economy and trade of the majority of the States which are now associated with the EEC developed in a hot-house atmosphere in a privileged relationship with the former metropolitan power—in this case, France. It was the same for Algeria, in a different juridical context, and for a few other African countries which are still dependent.

It was not possible, at the moment of the creation of the European Common Market, to abolish the existing bilateral advantages without causing grave damage, particularly to the African countries concerned which were approaching independence.

The aim of the association is to promote the economic and social development of the associated countries, while at the same time contributing to the expansion and liberalisation of world trade. In every way, trade is an integral part of general prosperity; its development must always be linked with economic and social progress.

It is on this basis, in relation to the historical facts, that the broad outlines of the system of association have been drawn. This necessarily implies various compromises between solutions at opposite extremes and between a position of established advantage and a forward-looking dynamism. It is therefore strongly criticised as being too illiberal by the non-associated countries, who do not share in the advantages of association, and as too little protectionist by the associated countries who are required to meet more and more the harsh conditions of the world markets

In essence, the commercial clauses in the system of association require a reciprocal liberalisation of trade between the Community and the associated countries in line with the principles laid down in the General Agreement on Trade and Tariffs (Art. XXIV). However, this liberalisation is asymmetrical in order to take account of the considerable inequality in present economic strength and in the standards of living found in one part or another. The associated countries may maintain or raise certain customs barriers against the Community either to aid their national budget or to protect their own production and, in particular, to promote industrialisation. In the absence of such clauses, the liberalisation of trade would certainly have hindered the development of the associated countries or, at least, would have directed it on the dangerous path of monoproduction of raw materials. In this way the system of association already represents an application, although within a limited geographical frame, of the principles accepted by the United Nations Conference on Trade and Development and enshrined in the General Agreement (Art. XXVI).

Does the initiation of free-trade areas between the Community and the associated countries imply the creation of a closed preferential system, simply an extension to the Six of the 'hot-house' relations which existed between many of the countries concerned and their former metropolitan power? On the contrary, the trade of the Community has, since 1958, developed to a greater extent with developing countries outside the association. That of the associated countries themselves has also diversified, especially with industrialised countries other than the Six.

The regulations of the association in themselves, moreover, provide the right of the partners to extend beyond the Six and the Eighteen measures of liberalisation of trade—provided these are not contrary to the principles of the association. As far as Africa is cncern ed, the associated states may even go so far as to grant to other developing countries, and particularly to their neighbours, trade concessions greater than those offered to the Six of the association by concluding with them customs or economic unions. The association, therefore, in no way forms an obstacle—neither in law, nor in fact—to closer economic co-operation between African countries.

As regards Europe, the Community may reach new agreements of association, as it has done with Nigeria. It also takes a constructive part in negotiations for the conclusion of a multilateral agreement on the lowering of customs barriers (the Kennedy Round) as well as in those aiming at the establishment of less erratic world markets (in wheat, cocoa, etc.).

In considering the efforts made on a world-scale to liberalise trade and to assure to developing countries outlets as wide and stable as possible, it is important not to lose sight of the temporary and evolving nature of the association. The rules for the liberalisation of trade contained in this system require many of the associated African states to make intense efforts as much in the internal organisation of production as in that of promoting external trade. They also manifest clearly the need for regional co-operation in Africa. The Community financial and technical aid to the associated states, also provided for in the system of association, strengthens the efforts of the African countries to diversify their economy and increase production. It should also help to fit them to play a full role in a world economy at once liberalised and rationally organised. Aid is thus, within the association, wedded to trade in the service of development.

Discussion

DISCUSSION was devoted entirely to considering the actual and potential implications of the Yaounde Convention and the system of association in their effect on African development. Some participants forcibly expressed the view that the form of association was designed to keep the African countries as primary producers, that it inhibited attempts to diversify their trading patterns and that it prevented regional development through customs unions linking associated with non-associated countries.

In reply Dr. van der Vaeren outlined the details of the Nigerian negotiations and explained how the Nigerian association differed from the EAMA form of association. The former was a commercial, trading agreement and the agreement did not include matters of technical aid or financial assistance. In addition, approximately 50% of the European Development Fund assistance to the Association has been devoted to the transport and infra structure sector—in other words, towards removing obstacles to industrialisation. Moreover, since aid is also given for import substitution (thus preventing the expansion of exports from the EEC to the African associates) and since the EEC has accepted that the tariff on the imports of manufactured goods from associated countries should be reduced to zero, it is difficult to accept the argument that the EEC is aiming to maintain the African associates indefinitely as primary producers.

The question of the diversification of trade was considered in some detail and the example of the reduction of the United Kingdom's share in Ghanaian trade since independence was used to illustrate the possibility of a developing country diversifying its trade. Dr. van der Vaeren made several comments on this general question. Firstly, the Yaounde Convention (Art. 9) provides for the formation of customs unions between associates and non-associates. Secondly, the acceptance by the EEC of the trade agreement and tariff reductions between Mali and the U.S.S.R. indicates the willingness of the EEC to allow tariff cuts to be made between an associate and an industrialised country outside the Community. Other examples were also furnished. Moreover, to assume that the Treaty of Association further divides the African countries assumes that existing divisions would disappear if the association were dissolved. This is an unjustifiable assumption.

Finally the general philosophy behind the association is to provide a transitional period in which the associates may be able to develop their economies so that at a future date they will be able to withstand open, world competition. By reducing the costs of production of certain commodities, and by being shielded from world competition whilst this is being carried out, the association provides a temporary phase between the colonial economic system, and future world diversification of trade.

Since the association is between the EEC as a group, and the individual African countries, acting as a block, the African associates should feel free to make full use of the opportunities available to them under the Yaounde Convention and accompanying institutions, to combat any unacceptable developments within the EEC relating to the form of association. In particular if European monopolistic firms exert too great an influence on the internal economic policy of associates, then the Yaounde Convention should be used to prevent this.

The UN Institute for Training and Research, and the Administrative Problems of Development

GABRIEL D'ARBOUSSIER

THE fundamental difference between a modern developing country and a traditionally underdeveloped country is the overriding attention paid by the former to economic growth. In consequence any policy decision in a developing country must pay heed to the demands of the future as well as determine the way in which it should be reflected in present-day action. In the majority of developing countries, the governments have worked out a plan that indicates the optimum pattern of economic development which appears possible by means of the economic policy instruments the government will be prepared to apply. The organisation of production and the distribution of products among the members of the community differ among countries, varying, in extreme possibilities, from a country with a centrally planned and operated economy to a country with a decentralised private enterprise economy. In most countries, this economic organisation is of an intermediate nature.

In view of the importance attributed to the future whenever a policy of economic development is adopted, the administration is called upon to perform new duties or devote more attention than in the past to,

> firstly, the administration of planning in government and industry; secondly, the administration of education and training intended for the nationals who are going to be responsible for the new industries—this includes the steps to be taken to facilitate the mobilisation of industrial personnel from outside the industry (the army, the civil service) or their

recruitment from abroad; thirdly, the administration of the departments and institutions through which the regular flow of development capital is ensured from domestic and foreign sources; and fourthly, the most efficient organisation of transfer of skills under the programmes of international technical assistance or co-operation.

It is well known from the experience of other countries, even those which have reached the highest stages of development, that the opening of a new line of production or marketing or the opening of a new enterprise meet with resistance on the part of buyers and consumers. To overcome this resistance the manager of a company is compelled to take measures which entail additional costs. This applies of course also to the new industries in developing countries. These costs must be faced however promising the long-range prospect of the new industry may be. It is for this reason that a government in a developing country frequently finds itself forced to take a more active part in industry. This is done either by offering special incentives to private producers or by undertaking the production for the government's own account, at least during the initial stages, before a market has been developed, and before the employees have acquired the skills which will enable the industry to face competition.

At this point it should probably be explained that when I speak about administration in connection with economic development, I do not limit myself to what is called in English 'public administration' but rather apply the word in the American sense where the word 'administration' applies not only to government administration but also to business administration or business management.

This is preferable because the most crucial problem of administration in all developing countries is the implementation of the national development plan which involves investment in human resources as well as investment in direct production and infrastructural facilities which are needed for the fulfilment of the plan. This is also preferable because the administrative difficulties which jeopardise development in government and business frequently are of a similar nature and therefore may be cured by the same remedies. It may also be that an obstacle to the expansion of production of an industrial product in private enterprises, such as restrictive business practices, may be overcome by establishing a competing public enterprise in the same industry; similarly, an obstacle to the expansion of production in a government plant, such as the lack of an adequate incentive, may be overcome by shifting the plant's production to a private industry.

From the very moment the United Nations was launched, the Organisation and its specialised agencies have taken an increasingly active part in the development policy of its member countries. The work of the United Nations in such fields as public administration, and the efforts to initiate the creation of public administration institutes, or the work done in the field of economic planning including the training of planning officials, are well known. Equally well known are the administrative problems which gave rise to these activities. It was only in 1962 that the administrative problems which arise in connection with development financing, and, as late as 1965, the administrative problems which arise in connection with the mobilisation of management, led to an initiative on the part of the United Nations to assist developing countries in their effort to overcome these difficulties by training senior officials from Africa, the Middle East and the Caribbean in these fields.

These activities are now part of the operations carried out by the United Nations Institute for Training and Research of which I am the Executive Director. I propose therefore to share with you some of our experience. It is my hope that it will throw a good deal of light not only on the difficulties experienced by the governments of new nations but also on the way in which these may be alleviated.

Development Financing

Not all economic development requires an increase in the capital-output ratio. Frequently the economic expansion is accomplished by the introduction of new production methods which require a capital input smaller than that considered necessary in the past. But in general the capital–output ratio increases as a result of the shift to more capital intensive industries. As a consequence, the government officials who were responsible directly for the development financing provided by the government itself, or, indirectly, for facilitating the flow of capital through the channels of financial institutions or in the form of direct investment, found themselves suddenly facing new tasks which went far beyond their past responsibilities. In many of the new countries the nationals who now occupy the senior posts in the financial administration had little experience of their own to draw on. This was because many of the senior posts in the Treasury used to be held by expatriates from the metropolitan country.

In the circumstances these nationals often find themselves without sufficient practical experience in the administration and planning of development financing, the fiscal and financial policies of government and the formulation of a development project including the assessment of its technical and financial requirements. Further, they need to learn what sources of funds are available from public and private financial institutions, and what are the measures which may be taken by the government to facilitate the financing of development projects from domestic sources. Last, but not least, they need to learn what are the sources of private foreign capital and how to obtain financial aid from abroad and what are the practical criteria and procedures governing the access to these financial resources.

When the United Nations has been able to provide training in these fields, it is largely by relying upon the willingness shown by the heads of foreign-aid agencies and private financial institutions to make available the services of their loan officers as tutors. They have also been willing to give of their own time to speak with the trainees themselves during the latter's visit to their agencies. Even when a foreign-aid agency or a bank is prepared to publicise up to a certain point the criteria which it will apply to evaluate the soundness of a development project for which a loan has been requested, still the final decision to be reached will depend on the special circumstances surrounding a particular application. They range from the resources available in the agency at the time, to the way in which the loan application is presented, the feasibility of the project under consideration, and the credit-worthiness of the borrowing country.

In the circumstances, nothing is more useful to the officials participating in such training than to learn from their tutors how well or badly other loan applications put forward in the recent past have fared. On this basis, they are thus able to draw their own conclusions. The examination of authentic application files which include the description of the project, its feasibilities studies and all relevant correspondence between the parties concerned will greatly help these officials to formulate similar requests in the future. When visiting the head of each agency, they are afforded an opportunity to penetrate further into the reasoning by which the loan agency arrives at its decision.

The United Nations has also been assisted by the managers of private industrial and construction firms who have lent their services as tutors and prepared textbooks describing the technical and financial preparation of development projects and the further steps by which they are implemented. Also valuable to the United Nations was the help given by high-ranking officials from developing countries who have a long experience as financial administrators, especially in matters of loan negotiations. On the basis of the experience they have gained within their own government departments they have dealt with financial planning and budgeting, the implementation of fiscal measures and the steps taken by their governments towards the establishment of financial institutions that would facilitate the accumulation of domestic savings. They also dealt with the question of borrowing from foreign sources and the way in which a developing country protects its interests in loan negotiations.

The relevant subjects covered by other tutors include the various ways in which developing countries attract direct investment from abroad for the new industries by setting up investment centres in the main industrialised countries, the creation of tax incentives, and the establishment of low-cost accommodation in industrial estates built by the local authorities. The response of the governments to this type of training programme seems to indicate that their participating officials have found it was of practical value to them in the performance of their administrative duties.

As described above, it is very much thanks to the tutoring assistance offered to the United Nations by its member countries that these officials have been given a full account of the success or failure experienced by other developing countries when implementing measures intended to bring about economic expansion. They were also given a complete and up-to-date description of the policies and administrative practices followed by financial-aid agencies and lending institutions in a great number of donor countries, and by international agencies. This may provide their governments with a wide variety of choices between alternative sources of capital. The programme reflects many viewpoints offered in turn by tutors belonging to all groups of member countries, East and West, North and South. It has also offered its participants ample opportunity to give an account of their own administrative problems and present their personal viewpoints. Thanks to this variety of views, these officials are able to return home with many alternative answers, thus offering their governments the choice of that answer which is found particularly suitable to the prevailing economic conditions and political climate of their country.

Mobilisation of Management

The implementation of any development project requires not only a sufficient amount of capital but also entrepreneurial skills. Skills in turn are the result of training and experience. Many years of training and experience are necessary to ensure that the people who will be in charge of the construction and subsequent operations of a new project will do an efficient job of it. Even in the case of a highly industrialised country, the head or manager of an enterprise cannot hope to develop adequate managing ability before he has gone through from 7 to 10 years of training.

In the common experience of developing countries, this only underlines the fact that the development plans call for industrial expansion which will require qualified managers in much greater number than can be recruited from among nationals who began to train 7 or 10 years ago or even earlier. This shortage cannot be overcome by increasing the number of people now being trained and given an opportunity to gain experience, since it will take years for those to be up to taking the responsibility of managing the new enterprises. One of the major reasons why loan applications are turned down is the inability on the part of the party who is seeking capital to assure the potential lender or investor of the adequacy of the management he would be able to secure for his new industry.

With a view to alleviating some of these difficulties it was decided that the United Nations would initiate training in the field of mobilisation of management. This training covers the steps which might be taken to bring nationals with training and experience from outside the industrial field (e.g. civil service, army) into the management of the new development projects. It also covers the steps which might be taken to mobilise foreign management personnel from more advanced countries. This may take the form of the simple recruitment of a foreign manager; a contractual arrangement with a foreign management agency; the utilisation of foreign management secured by a joint venture grouping nationals and foreigners in which the latter are responsible for the management; and management ensured through the admittance into the country of daughter companies which are fully owned and controlled by a foreign company. Attention is also paid to the different ways which make it possible to ensure the most economical use of the scarce managerial skills which are found at home or brought in from abroad by centralising them and making them available to co-operating firms or as a governmental service.

The government officials invited to participate in this training are those, who, in their countries, assume responsibilities for the mobilisation of management. They are usually senior officers from the ministries of finance who are, far more than any one else, conscious of the ill-effects of inadequate management, for it is their task to find the money to pay subsidies or to devise the ways and means to protect the new industries against foreign competition.

From the world of business, and from experienced civil servants, the United Nations has received the same type of assistance as for its training in development financing. Because of the poverty which prevails in most developing countries, the lack of private initiative and the inability on the part of the people of these countries to accumulate capital, plus the special cost of initiating new industries, it has been left to the states to take the responsibility for the implementation of development policies.

The nature of modern industry, in developing and developed countries alike, demands that, from the outset, an individual corporation should be given a form that permits it to enjoy economies of scale; that it should be operated in such a way as to make it able, under changing technical and economic conditions, to gain further economies of scale and—in a country with a decentralised priva-enterprise economy—achieve market dominance. In these circumstances, the attitude of many governments is the following: that it is through the successful operation of a public corporation that the road to industrialisation will be opened; that it is only through the government which, alone, has the command of the necessary financial resources, that a plant can be launched of sufficient size to benefit from low unit costs of production and marketing.

When it comes to finding the competent personnel to manage the public corporation, the government is faced with a number of problems. The type of management it is looking for differs in many ways from the management which would be most suitable in private industry. The government, although responsible for the fulfilment of the target of the plan, leaves the implementation of the plan to the head of the enterprises. As explained before, the planning, frequently, has to foresee heavy promotional costs to develop new markets and train inexperienced staff. In such a situation the current accounts will show losses which would be hard to justify in private industry. The persons who may be able to provide competent management are not available in a sufficient number, even if the government, although reluctant to do so, should decide to employ foreign managers as a stopgap measure.

This acute shortage of managers often leads to a situation where the government, by offering high salaries and large fringe benefits, may hope to attract competent people. Frequently, this offer of high salaries has the unfortunate consequence of attracting incompetent civil servants or relatives of the members of the government. This situation obliges the government to protect itself by establishing high recruitment standards of competence and efficiency. In many cases, these standards have proved difficult to enforce. It has also been the experience of governments that a failure to recruit competent managers either at home or abroad, has stood in the way of the successful implementation of a development programme. The ability of the country to absorb additional capital for further development may therefore be jeopardised.

In these circumstances, the government may seek a solution by engaging a foreign management agency which will provide management for a new industry in the initial stages against the payment of a fee. Many construction firms which have been responsible for the building of the plant are nowadays prepared to stay with the new venture beyond the turnkey stage and accept responsibility for running its operation up to a point when the government—or the private owner—are satisfied that its future is assured. This type of service is now provided by foreign plant builders from both East and West. Certain new companies even specialise in this kind of operation. In order to secure, on the part of the government—or the local private owner—and of the foreigners providing managers, an undivided interest in the success of the enterprise as well as ensure a steady flow of managerial skill and know-how, arrangements have been made in many cases to have the foreign corporation providing those services become part owner of the enterprise. The success of such arrangements depends on the extent to which they provide each partner with what he is seeking. At this point it should be remembered that the foreign partner also is interested in economies of scale and market dominance. For him, it is frequently of the essence that he be able to enter into new geographical and industrial avenues of expansion and cross political and industrial boundaries by enjoying the protection which only a joint venture partnership can offer.

One of the most effective ways in which management has been secured for developing countries has been through the establishment, by foreign enterprises, of wholly owned daughter companies. In spite of many obvious disadvantages of this form of industrialisation, there is no doubt that it has frequently made it possible to establish a new industry which would not, otherwise, have come into existence. The action required by the government of a developing country is, first, to bring into the country foreign corporations which are able to provide the necessary capital and, above all, the managerial skill and know-how, and, second, to take steps to make sure that both parties will continue to find their interests best served by the way in which the industry continues to operate. This may be done with a view to either transferring ownership to nationals of the developing country or gaining access to corporate reinvestment and additional know-how, inventions or experience.

In view of the limited size of their markets, the developing countries are particularly interested in managerial organisations which may enable small enterprises to benefit from the economies of scale. In many industries there is no advantage in having the manufacturing process proper carried out on a large scale. In these industries, considerable economies of scale can still be realised in such fields as research and marketing. Usually it is a definite advantage to have the marginal operations in these fields left to a centralised agency. This may take the form of either a technical consultation agency operated by the government for the benefit of the industry, or a joint sales and promotion corporation owned by a group of small-scale manufacturers, or even a co-operative sales agency operated for the benefit of the co-operating producers (or consumers) and at their expense.

In both the fields of mobilisation of management and development financing the administrative problems are manifold and extremely difficult to overcome. In many parts of the world the prospects of economic growth are indeed dim. However, the development plans which have been adopted by the government reflect not only their strong determination to develop but the desire to achieve this development within a minimum delay. It is for this reason that UNITAR has directed its training activities to fields such as mobilisation of management which would appear to lead to an early result rather than to that of training for management which can achieve its end only through a time-consuming process.

Technical Assistance

Shortage of technical knowledge and know-how in all fields of human endeavour, as wide apart as agriculture, health, education, industrial productivity, statistics, labour relations, etc., is well known to be a major bottleneck impeding the progress of developing countries, as much as if not more than the shortage of material resources. Technical assistance, or as it is now being called 'technical co-operation', a programme of sharing knowledge and skills between developed and developing countries, is therefore rightly considered a key factor in economic development.

The International Technical Assistance Programme of the United Nations and of its family of specialised agencies, in spite of its very small resources—which amounted to less than $150 million in 1965 for both the small-scale and short-term former Expanded Programme and for the projects, large in scope and duration, of the former Special Fund—has had a catalytic effect on the development of the recipient countries. It has in particular provided them with an imperative incentive to improve their administrative structure and to introduce economic development planning, in order to be able to plan also for the best possible use of the limited resources provided under the United Nations Technical Assistance.

It is natural under these conditions that improving the efficiency of United Nations Technical Assistance bodies and these training programmes, operated under their auspices since 1963, have been taken over by the United Nations Institute for Training and Research. Indeed they fall fully within the scope of the activity of the Institute, as they are directed both towards improving the efficiency of United Nations activities and assisting the recipient member countries. Moreover, in view of the subject-matter of this training, dealing with United Nations operations, it can be organised only within a United Nations framework.

Training in this field has been provided each year for a group of officials of recipient countries dealing within their governments with co-ordination of international technical assistance made available to these countries both on a multilateral and on a bilateral basis. The position of these officials within their respective governments varies in accordance with its particular structure. They may be located in the Foreign Ministry, the Prime Minister's Office, the Treasury, the Central Planning Organisation, whatever its name may be, etc. However, their duties and the difficulties they have to face are always the same: how to arbitrate between the conflicting claims of different technical ministries demanding each a maximum share of the available strictly limited resources in technical assistance, how to select from a multitude of various economic and social projects—which all of them appear useful and worth while—those whose impact on development may be expected to be the greatest and which therefore should be given the highest priority? Just as important, for achieving a maximum efficiency of technical assistance, is to solve in a satisfactory manner such questions as the prompt selection by the government of the most suitable candidates for experts amongst those submitted by the United Nations, as well as the nomination of the best candidates for fellowships. It is also part of their duties to keep under constant review all the technical assistance projects in operation, so as to check their continued usefulness and to determine whether they should not be terminated, in order to make funds available for the financing of more important ventures, etc.

In all these matters a close co-operation between these national co-ordinators and their United Nations counterparts, both in the field (resident representatives and their staff) and at the headquarters of the aid-giving agencies, is absolutely essential, in order to ensure the success of their common task of transfer of knowledge and skills. Such a co-operation implies a complete knowledge and understanding by each side of the problems, difficulties and methods of operation of the other. The Group Training Programmes now being operated by UNITAR have been geared towards achieving this objective of mutual understanding and thus of improved co-operation and efficiency. Rather than providing training in the strict meaning of this term, these programmes are intended to disseminate knowledge and information and to result in an exchange of experience and in a clarification by group discussion of common problems and difficulties.

In order to achieve these ends the group of about thirty participants in the Training Programme—organised this year for the first time on a bilingual basis, English and French—spends one month at United Nations Headquarters. They discuss there the different aspects of United Nations Technical Assistance—policies, co-ordination, administration, finance, procedures, etc.—with the officials of the United Nations Technical Assistance bodies (United Nations Development Programme and Bureau of Technical Assistance Operations) most competent in the respective fields. The participants also take advantage of this opportunity to discuss with the United Nations officials dealing with the national technical assistance programmes of their respective countries, or with individual projects concerning these countries, specific problems and issues relating to them. A similar method, including both group discussions of general technical assistance problems and individual interviews for settlement of practical national issues, is applied during the visits of the group for briefings at the International Bank for Reconstruction and Development and the International Monetary Fund in Washington, at the United Nations Specialised Agencies in Paris, Geneva and Rome and at the respective regional economic commissions of the participants.

After having taken over this year of training in United Nations technical assistance, UNITAR is going to enlarge both its scope and its variety. Thus, in order to take into consideration the needs of senior government officials, dealing with and interested in policies and planning of technical assistance, rather than in its implementation, UNITAR is organising, in addition to the regular Group Training Programme, for a small group of selected senior government officials, a one-month seminar on Major Problems of United Nations Technical Assistance. They will discuss in round-table meetings, with their colleagues in the United Nations and the specialised agencies, policy problems of Technical Assistance. A small group of deputy resident representatives of the United Nations Development Programme, for whom UNITAR is organising this year a special training programme, will also participate in the discussions of this seminar. The exchange of views and experience between the three categories of participants in these round-tables—the United Nations Technical Assistance officials, the deputy resident representatives, and their counterparts, the senior officials of recipient governments—is expected to be particularly enlightening and stimulating to all of them.

It is difficult to evaluate the useful impact of the training provided in the field of United Nations Technical Assistance. However, it is encouraging for us to note that the recipient governments, which are after all in the best position to assess these results, seem not only satisfied but most eager to have their officials benefit from this training. Thus the number of requests for participation has been steadily increasing and has reached this year more than double the available vacancies. This favourable reception by the recipient governments has been naturally the main reason for UNITAR's decision to expand its activity in this field.

The Civil Service and Development

A. L. Adu

As must have been emphasised over and over again at deliberations of the Seminar, the main concern of all new African states is to promote economic and social development, as a means of stabilising hard won independence and of raising the standards of living of their people to match their aspirations for greater prosperity after Independence. Political governments have their policies which they intend to carry through to fruition. Nevertheless, these policies cannot be instituted with any degree of assurance unless the governments are backed by an adequate and effective administrative machinery and an efficient civil service to operate this machinery. It is my object to concentrate on the role of the Civil Service in the field of development. Whilst most of the principles I may mention apply to all new African States, I intend to speak principally of those African States of British expression.

The essential role of the Civil Service, namely, that of being an executive arm of the government is one which, for the purpose of this discussion, I propose to take for granted. This is the traditional role of all civil services and is common ground to all states, be they developed or underdeveloped. I propose to concentrate rather on the special situation facing African States in organising their administrations and the peculiar problems which African civil servants have to grapple with. Some of these problems have been discussed at the conference already. They are, by all standards of estimation, complex and difficult and they face the African civil servant at a time when his repertoire of experience is severely limited. It is therefore worth looking at some of the historical developments which have applied to the public services in Africa, since, unless they are understood, it may be difficult to appreciate the gravity of the problems facing the African civil servant in his present role.

The Civil Service in newly independent African states bears a great deal of the qualities and handicaps of the Colonial Civil Service from which it has recently emerged. The Colonial Civil Service for all its reputation of arrogance and obstructionism provided a very effective administration for carrying out the policies of the government which created it. Its effectiveness could be judged by the fact that only a handful of men in the administration and police could control the whole state, maintain law and order, collect taxes and other forms of revenue and even carry through some economic and social development projects. It was, however, as its name implies, an essential instrument of colonial policy. Its senior ranks were filled by persons drawn from the metropolitan country and its structure was designed to carry out the policies and programmes of the colonial power. The fact that, in the few years prior to Independence, its ranks were opened to those of the indigenous peoples that possessed the necessary qualifications in education and experience, did not make any difference to its orientation or structure.

In its early stages the Colonial Civil Service was concerned principally with the maintenance of law and order and with the collection of revenue. The main core of the service was constituted therefore of the political administrative service of the police. There were other functional services, of course, such as agriculture, forestry, veterinary services, public works, lands administration, posts and telecommunications, health, education, and so on, but these were of minor importance compared with the political administration and the police.

The Civil Service in the present-day African state, however, is faced with tasks and responsibilities which were not envisaged in the pre-self government and pre-independence period. The accelerated constitutional development in the dependent territories caught the Colonial Civil Service unawares and the process of adjustment has therefore been hasty and difficult. All African states have had to concern themselves with programmes and policies, many of which were not within the competence or experience of colonial administrations of the past. They are all concerned these days not only with the consolidation of Independence, but also with the creation of nations out of tribes and racial groupings, the maintenance of security and stability, the creation of a welfare-state economy and the mounting of machinery for organising their countries' external relations. Most of these responsibilities were certainly not fully developed in the period prior to Independence.

The economic and social problems which the administration of any government has to tackle have already been discussed at this Seminar. It is therefore out of place for me to dwell on them, especially as in any case I am not competent to speak with any expertise on these problems. I wish to make only one general observation here. The African Civil Service, on the emergence of a country into Independence, very often is staffed by officers in its most senior ranks, from the metropolitan country which formerly ruled the new African state with only a small band of officers indigenous to the country in the lower echelons of the service. This small band of indigenous civil servants hold inferior positions in the Civil Service hierarchy, necessarily starting with little experience but with plenty of frustrated ambitions. The emotional tide immediately after Independence would carry them into key and policy advising positions and in this process they would replace expatriate experienced civil servants on whose knowledge and expertise the administration might have relied, but who nevertheless were an obstacle to the legitimate ambitions not only of the indigenous civil servants, but also of the clamorous public. Some of the expatriate staff would remain, but the Civil Service would have been reinforced by large numbers of untrained and inexperienced African officers and by new officers recruited from outside under various technical assistance projects.

It is in these circumstances that an African Civil Service has to grapple with the problems of stability without which economic development is difficult; with the problem of an agreed direction along which the nation moves and on which a development plan can be based; with the settling of the priorities for economic development; with the intractable problem of mobilising internal and external resources for development; and with the administrative problems connected with the gigantic effort of rapid economic advance. The economic role of the Civil Service is only part of the responsibility which it has to accept. For the purpose of the Seminar there is no need to dwell on the other aspects of Civil Service responsibility such as the administration of the Independence Constitution, the normal administration of the country, the management and policy direction of external relations of the country, and providing an effective amount of communication between the government and the people so that one could be translated to the other.

The African Civil Service has a unique role to play in its major task of economic and social development, since its members belong, or should belong, to a band of officers appointed on merit without regard to tribe or religion or race, which is dedicated to the vital responsibility of serving as an executive arm of the government of the day. Moreover, it is the one body that provides the national administrative grid for the maintenance of orderly administration and security throughout the State, one of the basic conditions on which development can be promoted.

It is in the light of this that we now have to consider the structure of the Civil Service necessary for its given role. The system that African states inherited is generally the hierarchical system which operates in the metropolitan country; for example, in the countries of British expression, the structure provides for the administrative class, executive and clerical classes; the professional and technical classes and the subordinate services. As I have explained earlier, the administrative class, or service, has provided the main framework of administration and is the body through which all policy decisions are taken or formulated. The professional and technical classes which, in the modern setting, provide the main impetus for economic scientific and technological development are, under this system, very much subordinate to the administrative class.

What is required in the modern situation in Africa is, in my view, a structure that is designed to facilitate the effective carrying out of the essential tasks of promoting social and economic development, of running economic services, handling external relations policies and dealing with all the other and complex issues and problems which plague all states in Africa these days. The dominant role of the generalist administrator, therefore, requires re-examination. An era of specialisation in various fields needs to be ushered in, with administration as only one of the fields of specialisation essential for running the affairs of the state. The new structure for the administration of the new African state should therefore be a structure related more strictly to the functional responsibilities of the government. Development planning, for instance, requires economic planning specialists, economic analysts, statisticians and so on, all of whom should be trained to understand the implications of policy and the management of affairs, an area of responsibility which should not be left entirely to the generalist administrator. Similarly, the development of other fields of government responsibilities, as for instance, economic services, agriculture, industry, engineering, scientific research, social development—all these require their own fields of specialisation with civil servants who not only have the expertise for the efficient performance in their specific fields, but also again have a general understanding of policy and management. The administrator has a role in his own field of political and financial policies, and responsibility for general co-ordination.

What I have in mind is that the new African Civil Service structure, in order to service the functions which the government of the state now has to discharge and administer, should provide room for the civil servant who has the peculiar functional specilisation required for each sector of the state's responsibilities. The administrator should be a member of the team of specialists, should fulfil his specialised role and should not necessarily play a dominant role. He would not necessarily be the team leader or head of the Ministry or department. The selection of this leader should be based on the criteria of merit and ability regardless of the original field of expertise or discipline of the individual. The leader must, however, be able to manage the team and to organise his political and administration policies within the framework of the political policy of his Minister and his government. In other words, the head of the Ministry or Permanent Secretary should be drawn not only from the administrative class but from any of the fields of specialisation on the basis purely of personal merit and ability.

On the question of organisation, African states have generally inherited the ministerial system introduced in the period of self-government by the imperial power. The arrangement of ministerial portfolios and of the content of portfolios, though of great importance to the whole organisation generally, nevertheless fall within the responsibility and discretion of the head of government, be he Prime Minister or President. Nevertheless, it has such impact on the organisation of the administrative machinery of government that it is the duty of the top civil servant, particularly the one occupying the position of head of the Civil Service, to give thought to the advice he should provide to his head of government for the better management of this important responsibility. It would make for greater efficiency if the subjects assigned to each ministerial portfolio were related subjects and could be constituted into a co-ordinated unit for easier administration. There is no necessity for me to go into detail as to the actual groupings of subjects which might provide for a more efficient organisation, especially as circumstances differ from one country to another and factors other than mere efficiency very often have their impact on decisions in this field.

It is important also to consider whether all the subjects which at present are included in the portfolios of Ministers for direct administration by civil servants should be so administered. In fact some of them could probably be best and more efficiently administered by bodies such as public corporations and other statutory bodies. Some may even be managed under private enterprise institutions, subject to appropriate regulation by the Ministry concerned. I have in mind, for instance, that research institutions, marketing organisations, public works and certain agricultural enterprises which in many countries are administered direct by Ministries are probably best handled by statutory corporations and private enterprise institutions. A decision as to what could be, or should be, handled in this way, must be left to the circumstances of each State and to the particular political circumstances of the governments concerned.

As a civil servant I may have tended to exaggerate the role which the Civil Service in the new African state does play and could play in promoting economic and social development. I am certain, however, that without the basic stable administration which—given the right policies of the political wing of the government, it falls to the responsibility of the Civil Service to provide—and without the right framework of structure and organisation which would ensure that the best use is made of such expertise as exists in the administration and such expert advice consultants as may be sought from outside the administration, the objectives of development cannot be easily attained. This, of course, calls for certain qualities from not only the Civil Service as a whole, but also from civil servants. As regards the Civil Service as a whole, one of the most important qualities is that it should be responsive to the national policies and the national aspiration. It should, whilst ensuring stability and orderly administration, get rid of the evils of bureaucracy and 'red-tapism' and should shake itself out of a sense of complacency and a feeling that its professional standards provide all the answers to any problem. This, of course, is easier said than done because it is in the nature of all Civil Services to be conservative and to resist change and dynamism. Fortunately in new African states the eagerness of governments to move ahead fast does not make it easy for the Civil Service to settle into a groove and run along that groove. Nevertheless, there is need for constant vigilence to ensure that the spirit of service in the administration is geared to the national aspiration as expressed in the political objectives of the government, and that this is one of the principal efforts of the government in its policies for economic and social advancement. I have said nothing in this talk about the political climate within which the Civil Service should function, although this is very important in the context of development.

In the ultimate, however, the quality of the Civil Service rests on the quality of the individuals comprising it and as it has been demonstrated in a few countries in West Africa recently, the quality of the individual civil servants could be important in giving impetus to development even under the most trying political circumstances. I wish to end, therefore, by posing certain principles by which, in my view, the good civil servant in the new African State might be judged. He must be judged by the way he uses his responsibilities. A civil servant should exercise his responsibilities and authority within limits that are acceptable to the nation as a whole. He must chiefly rely on elected representatives, that is, ministers and politicians to carry out the task of political policy decisions and control and direction of the administration. He must exist to serve the interests of the people and the service must therefore be open, in the sense of having wide contacts with the people. He must not operate in the selfish interests of the ruler or a directing class. He must be recruited without discrimination from a very broad social stratum on the basis of merit and ability. He must avoid an arrogant disposition. He must be controlled by public opinion and should not therefore be sheltered from the criticism of the press or organised public expression. He should not exist independently of political power, but he must not be completely subordinate to it. Whilst the Civil Service should operate with efficiency and loyalty and in consonance with the philisophy of the political party in power, its integrity should not be undermined by the party. The principle of continuity of administration should be maintained as also the anomymity of the Civil Service.

Discussion

ONE particular problem was emphasised by a number of speakers, viz. that the structure of the Civil Service was essentially colonial and, accordingly, ill-adapted to promote rapid economic advance. Such a service had low mobility and was overconcentrated in the national or regional capitals. There seemed to be little 'information gathering' preparatory to the compilation and execution of the Development Plan. The lack of contact between the administrator and the people of the rural areas often implied that there was no direct experience of the social and economic pressures involved in rapid development. Both Mr. Adu and M. d'Arboussier agreed largely with these comments: the Plan was often drawn up after the report of a visiting Survey Mission and later broken down into its local applications. In this way the agricultural problem tended to be neglected. The degree of communication between the top 'brain' and the bottom 'muscle' of development was thought to be of vital importance here and some institutions—for example, the army or political parties—could be used more extensively and effectively for this process. The successful experience in Ghana of the resettlement of villages displaced as a consequence of the construction of the Volta Dam was cited as an example of the value of research and documentation required in minimising the social tensions arising from rapid development.

The question of corruption and high standard of living among civil servants was raised. Mr. Adu paid a high tribute to the integrity of civil servants during periods of political disturbance and uncertainty. There was a general feeling that officials needed to experience higher living standards to be able to impart the motive for development to others. In order to counter any 'ivory-tower' mentality, officials should travel widely to examine the actual consequences of the operation of the development process.

There was some comment on the correct training required for the administrator. The interdisciplinary approach was stressed as an ideal and, in particular, the training of nationals in foreign countries was likely to be a useful counterpart to purely national training. It was felt, for example, that co-operation between francophile and anglophile states would improve if each understood better the system of government and administration of the other. Moreover, it was considered that the Ghanaian civil service showed a greater sensitivity to development following the post-independence recruitment of personnel from the technical agencies of the UN. Consequently it was desirable not to rely, as in the past, on the British system of a general administrator but to amalgamate where possible the expert with the administrator. The UNITAR Programme tends to concentrate on the higher officials and one of the best ways of maximising the value of their training is to place the official from the developing country in contact with his counterpart from a developed country.

The role of the administrator—expert in formulating the Development Plan was mentioned as a potential source of tension with the political structure of the country. This was perhaps indicated by overemphasis on the industrial sector of the economy with a relative neglect of the crucial need to raise the agricultural output. The difficulties involved in planning agricultural development were not minimised but it was felt that the employment (or advice) of social anthropologists in the planning department of the relevant Ministry, or the interdisciplinary education of the administrator (although this would reduce his expertise), would help to draw attention to the complexities of agricultural development and serve as a salutary counterweight to the relative optimism of the purely economic viewpoint.

Finally, the Seminar considered the reform of the administrative structure. Mr. Adu pointed out that much had already been done to adapt the colonial structure to the requirements of independent countries. Nevertheless, too much thought was in purely British or French terms. If the administrative machinery works reasonably well, then scarce resources should not be wasted on its reform.

Instead, such organisations as institutes of public administration might be invited to examine possible future adaptations of the Civil Service to developmental needs. M. d'Arboussier concluded the discussion by emphasising again that the present administrative structure often works to jeopardise what the country can, and does, gain from development. This thought should not be forgotten when the overall development plan is considered.

Problems of Rural Development

REPORT OF COMMISSION

THE problem of rural development was defined as the application of new methods of production so as to improve the existing techniques, to increase the productivity of the rural population and to raise their standard of living. The various aspects of the problem were considered under the following five heads:

1. Agricultural Production

The Commission noted the social and technical obstacles to increasing productivity which are associated with traditional subsistence agriculture; and with the objective of raising production, the Commission laid particular emphasis on the requirements of diversification and specialisation. This could be encouraged by governments through such means as the provision of transport facilities, technical advice, and marketing assistance. Those agricultural areas which have no special advantages would require more intensive development of modern methods of raising productivity —for example, the use of fertilisers and the application of new technology. The general objective of agricultural policy should be to encourage mixed farming, both to maximise the productivity of land and labour, and to develop crops to meet the different demands of domestic and foreign markets. The relative merits of the varying systems of land tenure were discussed, and the Commission recommended that, where appropriate, the basic existing system should be adopted when this would raise output; and in addition, when a change in land tenure is seen to be necessary, it should not be effected without the understanding and consent of the people. Governments should take all necessary steps to rule out the possibility of land speculation. Finally, the Commission stressed the importance of animal resources. Not only must every effort be made to raise the standard of domestic animals, but governments must recognise the potential of utilising wild animal resources.

2. Marketing of Rural Agricultural Products

The Commission examined the adequacy of existing marketing systems in meeting the distribution needs of producers. Marketing systems were regarded as having the following primary functions in African agricultural development: that of guaranteeing minimum prices, storing and distributing surpluses, providing the necessary infra-structure, processing where appropriate, and controlling the quality of commodities. In general it was felt that individual entrepreneurs (traders, merchants), and nationalised marketing boards were to be regarded as failing to fulfil these functions owing to a conflict between public and private marketing systems, the lack of co-ordination between producers and marketers at the local level, and inadequate credit facilities. It was thus considered that the organisation of producers co-operatives should be encouraged as they are the most effective link between producers on the one hand, and the demands of domestic, and foreign, distribution on the other (see also section 4, 'Capital Formation').

3. Social Policy

The Commission considered at some length the problems of community development, and labour problems associated with rural development. The conclusions are listed under these two headings.

(a) COMMUNITY DEVELOPMENT

This involved the use of various principles in implementing development projects. Essentially, the development agency must work through the existing units of society at the village level; decisions must be made at the local level using the traditional indigenous channels of communication, and national plans must take account of this; and this should be done by an agent who has first-hand experience of the new methods advocated by the agency, and who is familiar with local conditions and customs. Thus, in this way, the process of change is initiated by discussion, which has the following advantages: on the one hand, the people are able to see how the new techniques affect their way of life, and their values; those of high status can ensure that their positions are not undermined and in this way opposition to change is gradually overcome; on the other hand, during the discussion, the community decide which projects should be adopted, the project becomes 'our' project, and enthusiasm is generated to carry the project through to a successful conclusion. Finally, the new methods, through such discussions, are adapted to local conditions.

As a result of this process, the Commission felt that particular emphasis should be placed on the following features of rural development. African governments should understand the ways in which change occurs spontaneously in traditional society, and should work with, not against, the people. There should be a continual dialogue between the communities and the government, and national plans should be flexible enough to use ideas and enthusiasm generated at all levels. In addition, the new *élites* should be thoroughly acquainted with the principles of community development, by university teaching and by first-hand experience. A Minister of Rural Development, of Cabinet status, should be appointed to co-ordinate the various agencies implementing rural development programmes, and community development proposals should be an integral part of governmental policies in African states.

(b) LABOUR PROBLEMS

The Commission listed the factors which may induce low productivity of labour in the agricultural sector as high turnover and absentee rates, low levels of education, inefficient management, and unproductive equipment. The following remedies might raise labour productivity: by the education of rural workers in new techniques of production through farm schools, demonstrations, and extension work; by extending the comforts and benefits of urban living—e.g. health clinics, good schools, wider choice of food and consumer goods—educated people could be encouraged to work in rural areas. Moreover, where possible, secondary occupations in rural areas should be established: for example, pottery, weaving, and metal working. And perhaps one of the more significant methods available to reduce the harmful effects of the migratory worker is to reverse the social attitude which values the urban worker above his rural counterpart. In addition, co-operatives should be encouraged to create a more progressive organisation of the labour force, with regard for local conditions and the social structure. Finally, mention was made of the successful Masai experiment to indicate the peculiar problem of nomadic tribes.

4. Capital Formation

In the strict sense, with the exception of the production of cash crops for export, rural development is mainly relevant to capital formation within the country, and only minimally relevant to the important question of foreign exchange. The Commission recognised this limitation, and decided that the most direct contribution which can be made is that of the diversification of agricultural production, and in particular the production of import substitution foods. The earnings may be reinvested either through national marketing boards controlling prices, and thus transferring profits into the public sector; or by the encouragement of local farmers to purchase shares in co-operative societies or deposits in provincial savings banks. This latter view was preferred because of the favourable dynamic effect of successful co-operative societies on the local community.

5. Trade

From the point of view of the contribution of rural development to the trading sector of the economy, this was felt to be somewhat limited in the short-run, although its importance was greatly stressed. One of the contributions which rural development could make in the long run would be to remove the dependency of the economy on one exportable commodity—in other words, to diversify the export section of the agricultural sector; and as mentioned above, to reduce agricultural imports by producing for the domestic market. The obstacles to this policy were mentioned: the existing pricing mechanism, the fluctuations of world demand for primary products, the problems of the mobility of factors of production, and the need to hold down consumption in the expectation that what is saved will be invested. To assist this, and with a view to the revision of current trading arrangements, the Commission drew attention to the possibility of interregional trade agreements—e.g. an African Common Market and/or Customs Union; the need for world-wide agreements on commodity prices, production quotas, and tariffs; the benefits of increased research into marketing problems and advertising techniques; and finally the specialisation in industrial crops such as rubber, in meat hides and skins, and in timber, where there is the highest cost advantage.

The final point mentioned was that of the need to encourage the inflow of foreign aid, and in particular that such aid should be designed to increase the volume of trade, and in particular inter-African trade.

6. Other Points Raised

The refugee problem was regarded as a factor which could disrupt rural development plans, and cause a severe discrepancy between theory and fact in African development. Great attention should be paid to the work of the UN High Commissioner for Refugees, and of the national governments most concerned.

Chairman: T. E. MSWAKA, Ruskin College, Oxford.

The Commission also considered a background paper written by Mr. Archie Mafeje, Kings College, Cambridge, and the report of the 1965 Geneva Interne Programme on 'Rural Development'.

Co-operation in the impact of Technological Change

REPORT OF COMMISSION

Introduction

This topic was divided into four sections, each of which was introduced by at least two speakers from amongst the participants, followed by a general discussion. There was a certain amount of overlapping between the sections, but it was found that they formed a natural division allowing for some specialised discussion.

1. Transition from a Pre-technical to a Technological Society

The central theme for discussion under this section was the kind of technology which developing countries in Africa must choose in order to develop the peasant agricultural sector which is largely underemployed or totally unemployed. The discussion centred on a paper by Angus Hone of Nuffield College, Oxford, on 'Technologies and Economic Environments'.

In this paper it was pointed out that the major social problem concerned with technological change is the rapid increase in population and massive unemployment. While economic planning must as far as possible aim to solve population growth, it should also attempt to employ as many people as possible among those already born. The latter cannot be achieved by adopting the capital-intensive technologies of the West, whose emphasis is on labour-saving methods of production with the consequent substitution of machines for manpower. Large-scale labour-saving technologies constitute the least suitable method of production where the abundant resource is labour.

There are other reasons why capital-intensive technologies are not suitable for developing countries. The machinery introduced may be too expensive in relation to local incomes and savings capacity; large-scale production may not adapt to local market conditions. Many developing countries lack competent managerial and technical skills that are the preconditions for such a capital-intensive technology to work successfully.

Where labour is abundant, and supplies of capital and foreign exchange are scarce, there is a great deal to be said for implementing 'intermediate' or labour-intensive technologies. Intermediate technology could be brought about by

(a) purchasing second-hand machinery,
(b) using old designs of machinery,
(c) designing suitable labour-intensive machines.

In the discussion a wide range of views were expressed for and against the implementation of intermediate technology. Most participants felt that there were definite advantages to be gained from adopting labour-intensive technologies, in that they provide a more even distribution of income, besides solving the unemployment problem. A labour-intensive technology would also stop the mass exodus of people into towns with consequent social problems. It was emphasised, however, that since no country wants second-hand or obsolete machinery, for prestige reasons, the best method to bring about intermediate technology would be to design suitable labour-intensive machines that would, in effect, bridge the gap between the old and the new. Experience from war and space research shows that designing new equipment for 'new environments' could be done. The problem would be to persuade the manufacturers in developed countries to manufacture these new machines. Here international co-operation is most essential.

Objectors to the implementation of intermediate technology argued that the costs of establishing it had not been fully realised. If development efforts are to be scattered in rural areas, large investments would have to be made in roads and other parts of the communication system. The scattering of development projects would also mean that experts would have to move around; this would require large-scale technical assistance services. Labour-intensive technologies may, in addition, have a bad effect on the inflow of foreign capital. Traditional foreign investment has largely been in capital-intensive industries, because these have the highest rate of profit. This is precisely what foreign investors are interested in, and is something that a labour-intensive technology does not provide.

In conclusion, the general feeling among the participants was that there is a place for both types of technology in a developing country, but there is a greater need for labour-intensive technology for the development of the rural areas, at least during early phases of development.

2. Social and Cultural Aspects of Technological Change

The impact of technological change is primarily a social problem rather than a technical one, and involves changes in the social and cultural systems of people. It was recognised that the degree to which people are affected by such changes varies from one culture to another, because different communities react in different ways to social change.

All possible degrees of social and cultural changes exist in Africa today. Some communities are becoming totally adapted to European culture, while others do so only at work and not in their leisure time. The real problem arising from the introduction of technology is whether African countries should allow their social and cultural institutions to adapt to technological change in their own ways and at their own pace. It was the desire of most of the participants that in the process of technological change African countries should endeavour to preserve much that is good in their culture and not simply adapt foreign cultures. In this connection decisions and directions from the top are crucial. The common problem here is that little is known about the forces of change and how they affect the social and cultural welfare of people. It is difficult, therefore, to decide on the kind of innovations that would least disrupt established customs.

Cultural and social obstacles, as well as favourable factors and stimulants to technological change, were also discussed.

It was stressed that there is a great need to understand the cultural and social factors which could act as obstacles or stimulants to technological change. We need to understand the culture and social structure of small groups, because any form of social engineering must start at the community or tribal level. It is at this level that most technical assistance programmes seem to fail, usually because someone from outside is attempting to innovate change among people he does not really understand. Any given society will have forms of social, political, economic and religious organisations, and a set of values which will integrate as well as motivate most of their actions. Each social institution is linked with others and a change in one will usually precipitate a series of changes in other related institutions. There will be many factors in a society that will be barriers to change, but some of them may prove to be stimulants and favourable factors that will readily adapt to change. It is, therefore, best to work along the lines of least resistance in any society rather than try to change the impossible. People do not in principle resist change, in fact, they are changing all the time, and it is up to us to try and find out how we can best implement change. For this the sociologists and anthropologists can provide useful information and advise the planners. They may make blunders, but they will be less severe than those made by planners who do not understand the societies being dealt with.

The desire for a higher standard of living has provided one of the strongest stimulants for change. In many African countries today people are demanding change and it is rather embarrassing for governments because they cannot find the necessary capital to bring it about.

3. Education and Training

One of the major development problems facing Africa today is the lack and shortage of trained manpower at all levels. The schools which should be training people are themselves short of teachers. There are cases where teachers have been removed from schools to become diplomats and civil servants.

All levels of education are needed. In the past, however, the emphasis has been on university education with virtually total neglect of technical education. While university-trained people, such as doctors, lawyers, engineers and social scientists, will always be in great demand as countries prosper, development is not possible without middle-level skills such as technicians. Unfortunately, people tend to look down on technical education; it will require a great deal of effort and time to convince people that technical education is as equally important as university education.

African education is at present based mainly on the languages, techniques and values of European culture. This means, to a large extent, the adoption of a foreign culture and the abandonment of African traditional culture. In addition, the education system has little or no bearing on the geographical, cultural or historical facts of the countries in which these are taught. Participants felt quite strongly that all education should as far as possible be local, and should aim at preparing people for the environment which they are going to live in and develop. Exceptions to this were expressed for some professions, such as medicine, where it would be cheaper to train people abroad during the early stages of development.

It became evident throughout the discussions under the various sections that education is the essential and inescapable part of the development process and should precede any increase in physical development. If the African nations are to play their full part in development, they must have the level of education to *introduce, appreciate* and *adopt changes*. This is a condition *sine qua non;* technical assistance will not change the situation unless local educated people themselves participate in the development projects.

4. International Co-operation

Aid and technical assistance from Europe to the developing countries of Africa were the main topics discussed under this title of international co-operation. Some aspects of it were covered in the preceding sections.

The term co-operation has come to indicate some sort of agreement between countries for the promotion of reciprocal development in the contractual countries. Such agreements can be made between one country and another (bilateral) or between one country and several others (multilateral). The problem is to know which of the two is more likely to lead to rapid and efficient development—this being the main aim of co-operation, although other interests may at times obscure this. Multilateral forms of aid seem to be the best because they are less likely to have strings attached to them. Unfortunately only 10% of total world aid is in this form.

Some forms of aid have failed to achieve their purpose because of donor's competitiveness, commercial rivalry, aid-tying, high interest rates and sometimes political strings. Donor countries are too often interested in supporting prestige programmes with little relevance to the recipient's needs. Aid should be co-ordinated if it is to be effective. Some terrible examples of unco-ordinated aid were cited; for example, ploughs from the United States that were too large and heavy for the British tractors to pull in Malawi. The methods of the Alliance for Progress (Canada) were suggested as one way in which reasonable plans for co-operation to the best advantage of the recipient country may be organised.

Since the ability of a country to benefit from aid will depend to a great extent on the availability of skilled manpower of different types and grades, the main emphasis on aid should be on education, at least to begin with. Local people must be trained to implement development programmes.

Another form of international co-operation that was thought to be equally important is regional integration between the developing countries themselves. This might be in common services, such as research institutes working on common development problems. In practice this may not be possible, as experience has shown, for political reasons. But if countries realised that they are economically interdependent they might think more seriously about political harmony.

Chairman: L. K. MUGHOGHO, Magdalene College, Cambridge.

The Commission also considered a background paper prepared by John Burley, Seminar Organising Committee, Cambridge; and the paper by Angus Hone, Nuffield College, Oxford, on 'Technologies and Economic Environment'.

Afro-European Political Relationships

REPORT OF COMMISSION

WITHIN a broad discussion, the Commission concentrated on the movements of Pan-Africanism, and the growing economic links with the EEC. There was some disagreement in the Commission on the conclusions reached.

Pan-Africanism

Pan-Africanism is a general movement, partly the consequence of 400 years of European influence, and represents the effort of the African world to maintain its personality, and to adapt it to the present time. There has been a widespread misunderstanding about Pan-Africanism. It is not a doctrine of violence: its principle is to 'live and let live'. It does not seek to dominate the world, as other ideologies do, but is open to friendly relations which respect African dignity. It has manifested itself in a variety of forms, and has evolved considerably in the last few years. From the generic sense of solidarity among Africans, it has developed to represent a more concrete form of African unity. From the concept of 'negritude' we have now come to the concept of 'African personality'.

The political impact of Pan-Africanism has been the main cause of the formation of African states, and of their striving towards some form of continental unity. Some African leaders advocate a close co-operation between Africa and Europe. This co-operation, they maintain, is justified by the many ties which exist between the two continents. On the other hand, close links with Europe as a whole, or with single European nations, are thought to be dangerous by other African leaders, who see in them a threat to some fundamental African values. In particular, they fear a loss of cultural identity, and of political and economic independence. Relations with Europe, on this argument, should enjoy no special priority in the foreign policy of African states.

The strivings towards African unity in practice have had but partial success. The OAU has been established, but its functioning and political meaning are still quite limited. Pan-Africanism has found a first base, but still has a long way to go.

Africa and Europe

The slow pace towards Pan-African unity is thought to be mainly the result of the situation of close links with the dependence on Europe in which Africa found herself on the eve of political independence. It is a structural relationship, existing between individual African states and the former colonial power. This impairs action towards continental unity. It may well happen through no action of the European power, but as the indirect result of a *de facto* situation, and which is particularly shown by the association of the eighteen African countries with the EEC.

The agreement which involved the eighteen African states in the provisions of the Treaty of Rome was a consequence of post-colonial links. When these countries achieved independence, their association was renewed in the convention signed at Yaounde in 1964. And from the start it was France in particular which had been trying to get the other EEC members to include her former colonies into some kind of association with the Six. The highly integrated nature of the economic links between France and her colonies existing prior to independence eased the transitional period to a new form of relationship, but to some extent the association is the economic continuation of the colonial past. From a political point of view, what should be stressed here is the fact that the associated members were somewhat forcibly drawn into a Western Grand Design constituting a united Europe which, in partnership with the U.S.A., would be the main pillar of western defence. As far as the associated members are concerned, these political aims have never been specifically stated. They nevertheless command the political thinking of some of the leaders of the eighteen states, and this in spite of the neutralist creed which these leaders profess. The Commission thus felt that, from a political point of view, the association of African states with the EEC is a stumbling-block on the road to neutralist Pan-African unity.

From the purely economic standpoint, there is no denying that the association with the EEC has brought some advantages to the African associates, especially in increasing the flow of multilateral aid through the EIB and the EDF. It is probably too early to see how far this aid has substantially changed the 'colonial structure' of the economics of the associates, although there has been little indication so far of any real change. It is clear that efforts should now be made to increase the bargaining power of the associates in their negotiations with the EEC, and in particular to concentrate on stabilising the export prices of their commodities, and to increase the productivity of their manufacturing industries so as to be able to sustain competition on the wider European and world markets. This should be done in conjunction with the other developing countries, within the framework of the UN Conference on Trade and Development, the GATT agreements, and the Kennedy Round negotiations.

The Commission also took notes of the existence of active co-operation between non-aligned European states and the developing countries of Africa. The example of Yugoslavia, and in particular her project in Ethiopia, was mentioned favourably. It was pointed out that active peaceful coexistence and co-operation can develop between states irrespective of their social and political systems, and that this coexistence and co-operation are indispensable for peace and progress in the world.

Finally, the Commission advocated the creation of an African Common Market, which would lead to an increase in inter-African trade, and enable the African states to harmonise their investment policies and act collectively together in their dealings with the outside world.

Chairman: S. KACHAMA-NKOY, Queen Elizabeth House, Oxford*

The Commission also considered a background paper on the subject of Afro-European political relationships prepared by Miss Barbara Hoffman, of LSE.

*The sad and untimely death of Stefan Kachama-Nkoy in 1968 has come as a great shock. His vivid mind and colourful personality will always be remembered by the participants of the Seminar—Eds.

Bibliography

1. *African Development*

ALLAN, W.: *The African Husbandman.* Edinburgh, 1965.
BOHANNAN, P. and DALTON, G. (Eds.): *Markets in Africa.* New York, 1965.
DUMONT, R.: *False Start in Africa.* London, 1966.
ECONOMIC COMMISSION FOR AFRICA: *Economic Survey of Africa since* 1950. 1959.
FRIEDLAND, W. H. and ROSBERG, C. G. (Eds.): *African Socialism.* Standford, 1964.
INTERNATIONAL ECONOMIC ASSOCIATION (Ed. E. A. G. ROBINSON): *Economic Development for Africa South of the Sahara.* London, 1964.
HAZLEWOOD, A. D.: *The Economy of Africa.* London, 1961.
JACKSON, E. F.: *Economic Development in Africa,* Oxford, 1965.

2. *Political Aspects of Development*

CARTER, G. M. (Ed.): *African One Party States.* Cornell, 1962.
COWAN, L. G.: *The Dilemmas of African Independence.* New York, 1964.
PADELFORD, N. and EMERSON, R. (Eds.): *Africa and World Order.* New York, 1963.
ROYAL INSTITUTE OF INTERNATIONAL AFFAIRS: *The EEC and African Associated States* (mimeo). London, 1963.
THIAM, D.: *The Foreign Policy of African States.* London, 1965.

3. *List of Related Publications*

Attention is drawn in particular to the following publications:

Africa Research Bulletin: Monthly—Economic, Financial, Technical Series;
—Political, Social, Cultural Series.

1 Parliament Street, Exeter.

The Overseas Development Institute (160 Picadilly, London, W.1) publish pamphlets and short monographs on various aspects of development, and aid, including a series on British Aid, and individual pamphlets on German, and French, Aid.

UN Economic Commission for Africa: Bulletin—Quarterly;
Conference Publications.

Addis Ababa, Ethiopia.

Reports of Missions of the World Bank to various countries.
International Bank for Reconstruction and Development,
1818 High Street, Washington D.C., U.S.A.

For more detailed studies of specific countries, most governments publish Plans, copies of which are available from the relevant Ministry.

4. *Bibliographies*

CARTRY, M. and CHARLES, B.: *L'Afrique au Sud du Sahara: Guide de Recherches.*

CONOVER, H. F.: *Africa South of the Sahara: A Select Annotated List of Writings*. Washington, 1964.

FORDE, C. D.: *Select Annotated Bibliography of Tropical Africa.* New York, 1956.

HAZLEWOOD, A. D.: *The Economics of Underdeveloped Areas* (2nd ed.). London, 1959.

HAZLEWOOD, A. D.: *The Economics of Development.* London, 1964.

Index